HOLL
HOMES

POSTCARD VIEWS OF THE EARLY STARS' ESTATES

Mary Martin Postcards,
Tina Skinner,
& Tammy Ward

Schiffer Publishing Ltd

4880 Lower Valley Road, Atglen, PA 19310 USA

Library of Congress Cataloging-in-Publication Data

Hollywood homes : postcard views of the early stars'
estates / [compiled] by Mary Martin Postcards, Tina
Skinner & Tammy Ward.
    p. cm.
    ISBN 0-7643-2202-8 (pbk.)
1. Motion picture actors and actresses—Homes and
haunts—California—Los Angeles—Pictorial works. I.
Skinner, Tina. II. Ward, Tammy. III. Mary Martin
Postcards.

PN1993.5.U65H593 2005
791.4302'8'092279494—dc22
                                    2004029868

Designed by Mark David Bowyer
Type set in Caslon224 Bk BT/Souvenir Lt BT

ISBN: 0-7643-2202-8
Printed in China
1 2 3 4

Published by Schiffer Publishing Ltd.
4880 Lower Valley Road
Atglen, PA 19310
Phone: (610) 593-1777; Fax: (610) 593-2002
E-mail: Info@schifferbooks.com

For the largest selection of fine reference books on this
and related subjects, please visit our web site at
www.schifferbooks.com
We are always looking for people to write books on new
and related subjects. If you have an idea for a book
please contact us at the above address.

This book may be purchased from the publisher.
Include $3.95 for shipping.
Please try your bookstore first.
You may write for a free catalog.

In Europe, Schiffer books are distributed by
Bushwood Books
6 Marksbury Ave.
Kew Gardens
Surrey TW9 4JF England
Phone: 44 (0) 20 8392-8585; Fax: 44 (0) 20 8392-
9876
E-mail: info@bushwoodbooks.co.uk
Free postage in the U.K., Europe; air mail at cost.

Introduction

Even before "talkies" took root in theaters around the nation, tourists to the West Coast paid guides to drive them past homes of the silent screen idols. Besides a chance to gawk at the finery fame could afford, hope hung in the air that one might catch a glimpse of a big-screen idol peeking from behind a curtain or perhaps just heading out the door to some deliciously exclusive, socialite affair.

The homes the stars built in the first half of the 20th Century are almost modest by today's standards. Many are smaller than homes built today on middle-class incomes. Tudors, Spanish Colonials, and such basic styles sufficed, while later stars flirted with "moderne" design. Still, the appeal was, and still is, the star power that emanated from within these abodes, rather than the earthy substances of which the mere structures were composed.

This story, told through the facades of their home, explores the lives and careers of the newly famous stars, many who made their first mark in the medium of silent screen, and on through the survivors of the talkies. These are the early megastars, who lived within an aura of magic and captured the imagination of a nation. These homes were built during the golden era of the silver screen, when theaters were spreading like wildfire across North America, and bringing with them the beautiful faces and charming plotlines generated during Hollywood's formative years.

[c. 1930s; $5-10]

[c. 1930s; $5-8]

[c. 1940s; $5-8]

Three "colonies" of movie star and celebrity homes acted as magnets for tourists, as pictured here. The Malibu Beach card was postmarked 1939 from Long Beach and sent to someone in Maine. The card featuring the movie stars homes in Pacific Palisades in Santa Monica was never used. The card picturing homes in Hollywood Hills was postmarked 1955 from Whittier, California, and mailed to Massachusetts.

Abbott & Costello

Home of Bud Abbott, Encino, California and home of Lou Costello, North Hollywood, California.
[c. 1940s; $5-8]

William Alexander "Bud" Abbott (b.1895 - d.1974). Bud Abbott dropped out of school in 1909 and worked as a manager and/or a treasurer for various theaters around the country. In 1931, he began his famous partnership when he substituted for Lou Costello's straight man. The pair toured nationally until a spot on the *Kate Smith Hour* gave them the exposure they needed to sign with Universal for their first movie, *One Night in the Tropics* (1940). Abbot and Costello enjoyed a 21-year duo career that spanned burlesque, Broadway, radio, films, and, finally, television.

Louis Francis "Lou" Costello (1906-1959). Lou Costello grew up in Paterson, New Jersey. His athletic prowess earned him a scholarship to Cornwall-on-Hudson Military School, but he left to pursue a performing career before graduation, doing stunt work in Hollywood. In the mid 1930s he started making a name for himself as a burlesque comedian. Costello's ambitions drove the Abbott/Costello duo beyond the stage, toward his dream of starring in movies. Abbott and Costello enjoyed a decade as Hollywood's biggest moneymaking team. In 1956, Costello went solo and enjoyed fair success in nightclubs and television acts until his death three years later.

May Allison

Home of May Allison, Hollywood. [c. 1930s; $4-7]

May Allison (b.1890 - d.1989). A delicate-looking blonde, May debuted in *A Fool There Was* in 1914, but made her mark as partner to leading man Harold Lockwood in a series of World War I romances. She was married to her husband James Quirk, who was an editor for *Photoplay Magazine,* until his death in 1932. Besides her film career, May Allison is known for being an editor with *Photoplay Magazine* after her husband's death and for her patronage of the Cleveland Symphony Orchestra.

Don Ameche

783   HOME OF DON AMECHE. NORTH HOLLYWOOD. CALIF.

Home of Don Ameche, North Hollywood. [c. 1940s; $5-8]

Don Ameche (b.1908 - d.1993). This ever-smiling Hollywood leading man got his start on radio on *The Chase & Sanborn Hour*. His baritone voice lent itself to many leading musical film roles of the 1930s and '40s. He did a lot of television work in 1950s variety shows, and later made a highly successful comeback as a geriatric character actor in *Trading Places*. His role in *The Story of Alexander Graham Bell* (1939) spawned the long-standing Hollywood in-joke about Ameche inventing the telephone and the expression, "You're wanted on the Ameche," as a way of telling someone they had a phone call.

[c. 1930s; $10-15]

DON AMECHE   PARAMOUNT

6

Eddie "Rochester" Anderson

852—Home of Eddie "Rochester" Anderson, Los Angeles, California

NBC Comedian and Screen Star

1B-H1019

Home of Eddie "Rochester" Anderson, Los Angeles. [c. 1940s; $5-10]

Eddie "Rochester" Anderson (b.1905 - d.1977). The son of a minstrel performer and a circus tightrope walker, Anderson entered show business himself at age 14 with a song-and-dance act. His movie career began in the 1932 *What Price Hollywood?* In 1937, Anderson was engaged to play a one-shot role as a railway porter nicknamed Rochester on *The Jack Benny Program*, and was an instant hit, becoming a regular on Benny's radio programs and in his movies.

Jean Arthur

62684

Home of Jean Arthur, Beverly Hills.
[c. 1940s; $5-7]

Jean Arthur (b.1900 - d.1991).
Graduating from silent films, Arthur's
comedic squeaky voice helped
launch her overwhelming fame in
the 1930s. Her big breakthrough
came in *The Whole Town's Talking*
(1935). She starred in dozens of
films including *Mr. Deeds Goes to
Town*, *Mr. Smith Goes to Washington*, and *Shane*. Her fame ebbed in
the 1940s and '50s, and in 1966,
The Jean Arthur Show lasted only
eleven weeks on television.

[c.1940s; $15-20]

Gene Autry

849—Home of Gene Autry, North Hollywood, California

OB-HS11

Home of Gene Autry, North Hollywood. [c. 1940s; $5-10]

Gene Autry (b.1907 - d.1998). America's favorite cowboy, Autry enjoyed an incredible stretch of fame during the 1930s and '40s as movie star, radio star, recording star, and Academy Award-nominated songwriter. Born Orvon Autry, he was working as a telegraph operator in the 1920s when Will Rogers overheard him singing and convinced him to give show business a try. By the early 1930s he had his own radio show, "National Barn Dance," and was a leading recording artist with Columbia Records. Autry entered the film industry in 1935 and made dozens of movies in the Western genre. He became the only Western actor ever to make the list of Hollywood's top ten attractions in the early 1940s. During World War II, he served as a flight officer, and his popularity was only slightly diminished by his absence. In 1954, he retired from movies, leaving behind a legacy of 200 best-selling songs he wrote, including the well-known seasonal song *Here Comes Santa Claus*. He did some television work in the 1960s, and published his autobiography, *Back in the Saddle Again*, titled after his signature song.

[c.1930s; $8-10]

9

Lauren Bacall

Home of Lauren Bacall, Bel-Air. [c. 1950s; $5-7]

Lauren Bacall (b.1924 -). A former model, Bacall's career was launched when her image appeared on the cover of *Harper's Bazaar* magazine and director Howard Hawks picked her to be his "fresh" star. She debuted with Humphrey Bogart in *To Have and Have Not*, and her deep, throaty voice helped obscure her youth and added to the sultry image she created on-screen. She and Bogart went on to make three more films, and they were married in 1945. On her own, she made her mark in *How to Marry a Millionaire* (1953), *Designing Woman* (1957) and *The Gift of Love* (1958). Bacall made a comeback after a lull in the 1960s, with the stage production *Applause* (1970), a musical adaptation of *All About Eve*. She continues to excel in film roles.

[c.1980s; $4-6]

Lucille Ball and Desi Arnez

Lucy Ball's Palm Springs Home

Home of Lucille Ball and Desi Arnaz, Palm Springs. [c. 1950s; $4-6]

Front and back views of home of Lucille Ball and Desi Arnaz, Beverly Hills. [c. 1950s; $4-6]

[c.1980s; $4-6]

Lucille Ball (b.1911 - d.1989). American TV's most popular comedienne for over a decade, Lucy was known for her blazing red hair and slapstick situation comedy gags. She starred in five different TV shows during her career; the original, *I Love Lucy* (1951-57) was consistently number one in the ratings and continued in reruns for decades. *I Love Lucy* also starred Ball's real-life husband, Cuban bandleader Desi Arnaz; the couple had two children, Desi Jr. and Lucie. Together they founded a successful TV production company known as Desilu.

Desi Arnaz (b.1917 - d.1986).
Married to Lucy both on and off screen, Desi was best known as her television partner Ricky Ricardo. Born in Santiago, Cuba, Desi got his start as a musician, then leader of a mixed Latin-Cuban big band that helped to popularize the conga. His success in the Broadway musical *Too Many Girls* led to a role in the film version, and a Hollywood career, and marriage to comedienne Lucille Ball.

John Barrymore

HOME OF JOHN BARRYMORE, HOLLYWOOD, CALIF.   A83

Home of John Barrymore,
Hollywood. [c. 1930s; $5-7]

BEVERLY HILLS, CALIFORNIA

Residence of Mr. and Mrs.
John Barrymore (Dolores
Costello), Beverly Hills.
[c.1930s; $5-7]

c.1920s; $12-15

John Barrymore (b.1882 - d.1942). Appearing in about
sixty films and dozens of stage and radio productions,
John Barrymore is considered one of the most idolized
performing arts figures of his generation, crowned by his
title role in stage performances of *Richard III* (1920) and
Hamlet (1922-25). Born in Philadelphia, he first tried his
hand at painting and fine art before turning to the stage.
His film debut in 1903 launched him as a matinee idol.
His elder brother and sister, Lionel and Ethel, were also
performers, and the three performed together once, in the
movie *Rasputin and the Empress* (1932). The story of the
Barrymore family is related to some extent in the movie
The Royal Family (1934), a play by Edna Ferber and
George S. Kaufman.

Warner Baxter

6A-H2541

Home of Warner Baxter, Bel-Air. [c. 1940s; $5-7]

Warner Baxter (b.1889 - d.1951). In a reprise of the great American story, Ohio born Baxter moved at age nine with his family to San Francisco to start a new life. In his teens, the great earthquake left them homeless. He launched his vaudeville career as a young man in 1910, and landed his first starring film role as the Cisco Kid in the film entitled *In Old Arizona* (1929). This earned him the Academy Award for Best Actor, and by 1936 he was earning the highest salary of any actor in Hollywood. However, by 1943 he had slipped to B movie roles. Crippling pain from arthritis led him to a drastic lobotomy procedure, and he died shortly afterward of pneumonia.

WARNER BAXTER.

c.1920s; $12-15

14

HOME OF WARNER BAXTER, BEL-AIR, CALIFORNIA

T 265

60138

Home of Warner Baxter, Bel-Air. [c. 1940s; $5-7]

Wallace Beery

THE HOME OF WALLACE BEERY, BEVERLY HILLS, CALIFORNIA

T196

Home of Wallace Beery, Beverly Hills. [c. 1930s; $5-7]

HOME OF WALLAC

62692

Home of Wallace Beery, Beverly Hills. [c. 1940s; $5-7]

RESIDENCE OF WALLACE BEERY, BEVERLY HILLS, CALIFORNIA

810

Home of Wallace Beery, Beverly Hills. [c. 1940s; $5-7]

WALLACE BEERY

[1930s; $12-15]

Wallace Beery (b.1885 - d.1949). Beery started show business first in the circus and then in Broadway musical variety shows. In 1913, he moved to Hollywood, and two years later starred with Gloria Swanson in *Sweedie Goes to College*. After a short-lived marriage to Swanson ended in allegations of abuse, he began to play the heavy in movies. He was nominated for the Best Actor Academy Award for his role in the 1930 prison film *The Big House*. Other notable films included *The Champ* (1931) and the role of Long John Silver in *Treasure Island* (1934).

Constance Bennett

Home of Constance Bennett, Beverly Hills. [c. 1930s; $5-7]

Constance Bennett (b.1904 - d.1963). The eldest of three daughters born to theatrical luminary Richard Bennett and his wife, actress Adrienne Morrison, Constance became one of Hollywood's highest-paid performers during the depths of the Depression in the early 1930s. Bennett entered films at age seventeen and became a leading lady of Hollywood silent films. She was a hit in the lavish musical comedy *Moulin Rouge* (1934). She paired well with Clark Gable in *After Office Hours* (1935) and *Ladies in Love* (1936), and with Cary Grant in her most memorable film, *Topper* (1937).

[c.1930s; $12-15]

CONSTANCE BENNETT

18

Enid Bennett

794:—Enid Bennett's Home, Beverly Hills, California

Home of Enid Bennett, Beverly Hills. [c. 1930s; $5-7]

Enid Bennett (b.1893 - d.1969). This Australian-born actress was one of the pioneers of the silent screen. She was featured in over fifty productions, including the role of Lady Marian opposite Douglas Fairbanks in *Robin Hood* (1922). She was married to actor/director Fred Niblo, Sr. and later to director Sidney Franklin. She made several films after the introduction of sound, including *Strike Up The Band* (1940), with Judy Garland and Mickey Rooney. She retired from movies in order to devote more time to her three children.

Jack Benny & Sadie Marks

Home of Jack Benny, Beverly Hills. [c. 1940s; $5-7]

Home of Jack Benny, Beverly Hills. [c. 1940s; $5-7]

John Hughes Photo

Home of Jack Benny and Sadie Marks, Beverly Hills. [c. 1940s; $6-8]

Home of Jack Benny, Beverly Hills. [c. 1950s; $4-6]

Jack Benny (b.1894 - d.1974). Born Benjamin Kubelsky in Illinois, he worked as a vaudeville violinist in his early twenties. After a stint in the Navy, he returned to the stage, this time as a comedian. He entered motion pictures in 1927, and in 1932 launched an enormously successful radio career. Benny's comedic style was unique, allowing the talented actors around him to get the laughs at his own expense. In the 1950s Jack Benny worked in both radio and TV until 1955, continuing with television until 1965.

Sadie Marks (b.1905 - d.1983). Sadie and Jack Benny met while he was traveling with his vaudeville act, and they married in Waukegan in 1927. Her character, Mary Livingstone, first appeared on the radio program as the president of the Jack Benny Fan Club in 1932. Her wild laugh and quick wit became inseparable from the radio show, and eventually she legally changed her name to Mary Livingstone.

[c. 1960s; $10-12]

Monte Blue

Home of Monte Blue, Beverly Hills. [c. 1930s; $4-6]

Monte Blue (b.1890 - d.1963). Blue was part-Cherokee and a product of the Indian orphanage system. He broke into Hollywood as a movie-studio handyman in the early 1910s, climbing through the ranks as extra, stunt man, and finally as a dependable box-office attraction in leading roles beginning in 1915 through the 1920s. He played everything from lawyers to baseball players. Later he carried supporting roles and stayed busy in Westerns, extending his activities into TV. Blue continued accepting character roles until retiring from acting in 1954.

Monte Blue as Abner Elliott. [c. 1930s; $6-8]

23

John Boles

Home of John Boles, Hollywood. [c. 1940s; $5-7]

JOHN BOLES' RESIDENCE, HOLLYWOOD, CALIFORNIA

HOME OF JOHN BOLES, BEVERLY HILLS, CALIFORNIA   T-370

Home of John Boles, Hollywood. [c. 1940s; $5-7]

JOHN BOLES

John Boles (b.1895 - d.1969). This animated baritone was rumored to have been an Allied spy in Europe and Turkey during World War I. He made his screen debut in a silent film *So This is Marriage* (1925), but he was shown to better advantage in talking pictures, beginning with the 1929 musical blockbuster *Rio Rita*. He was much in demand in the early 1930s until his film career wound down in 1943.

1930s; $8-10

Hopalong Cassidy (Bill Boyd) and Dorothy Sebastian

Home of Hopalong Cassidy, Palm Springs.
[c. 1950s; $5-7]

MR. AND MRS. BILL BOYD (DOROTHY SEBASTIAN) HOME, 525 NORTH ARDEN DRIVE, BEVERLY HILLS, CALIF.   BH13

BEAUTIFUL HOMES OF SOUTHERN CALIFORNIA

Home of William "Bill" Boyd and Dorothy Sebastian, Beverly Hills.
[c. 1930s; $5-7]

[1930s; $8-10]

William Boyd "Hopalong Cassidy" (b.1875 - d.1972). Boyd worked as a manual laborer before breaking into the movies in 1919 as an extra. He was a favorite of Cecil B. De Mille, cast as an unassuming leading man in comedies and adventure films. Boyd experienced a setback over a scandal concerning another actor with the same name. His career took off again in 1935, when he began to appear in *Hopalong Cassidy* films based on the Clarence E. Mulford stories of the Old West. Boyd, as Hopalong Cassidy, became a Western icon and a virtual endorsement industry.

Dorothy Sebastian (b.1903 - d.1957). From the chorus ranks of Broadway, Alabama-born Dorothy Sebastian was recruited for films in 1925. The high point of her brief starring career came when she was teamed with Joan Crawford and Anita Page for a popular series of MGM romantic dramas. She was also well received in *Spite Marriage* (1929), wherein she was cast opposite her then-lover Buster Keaton. They were reunited years later in the low-budget comedy *Allez Oop* (1935). Sebastian went into semi-retirement in the mid-1930s after marrying Bill Boyd just before his rise in the role of Hopalong Cassidy. They divorced shortly afterward in 1936.

George Brent

HOME OF GEORGE BRENT. BEVERLY HILLS. CALIFORNIA   T-369

Home of George Brent. Beverly Hills. [c. 1940s; $5-7]

George Brent (b.1904 - d.1979). One of Hollywood's most dependable leading men, the handsome actor played opposite all of Warner Brothers greatest actresses, including Barbara Stanwyck, Olivia de Havilland, and Bette Davis. He began his career playing small roles as a child in Abbey Theater (Ireland) plays, then toured Canada and New York with stock companies. He worked on Broadway in the late '20s, before heading for Hollywood to begin a career that spanned two decades. He starred in the TV series *Wire Service* from 1956-59, and made his final screen appearance as a judge in *Born Again* (1978).

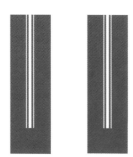

Fanny Brice

828—Residence of Fanny Brice, "Baby Snooks", Bel Air, California

OB-HS14

Home of Fanny Brice, Bel-Air. [c. 1940s; $5-7]

Fanny Brice (b.1891 - d.1951). The original "Funny Girl," this comedienne launched her career at local amateur night shows in New York, and then joined the vaudeville circuit where she made her mark with her ethnic songs. She went on to appear in virtually every edition of *The Ziegfeld Follies* from 1911 to 1925, and headlined a 1933 revival. She did not translate well to the big screen, but excelled on stage and radio.

Joe E. Brown

809 RESIDENCE OF JOE E. BROWN, BEVERLY HILLS, CALIFORNIA

6A-H995

Home of Joe E. Brown, Beverly Hills.
[c. 1940s; $5-7]

Joe E. Brown (b.1892 - d.1973). At ten years of age Brown joined a circus tumbling act and started his vaudeville career, climbing to Broadway in 1920 as a comedian in an all-star review, and finally to Hollywood in 1928. His trademark was his huge grin, and his best films included *Fireman Save My Child* (1932), *Elmer the Great* (1933), and *Alibi Ike* (1935). He played flute in an adaptation of Shakespeare's *A Midsummer Night's Dream* (1935). After this he starred in a series of largely disappointing low-budget comedies for independent producer David Loew. He then worked tirelessly entertaining troops around the world during World War II.

Bob Burns

Home of Bob Burns, Bel-Air. [c. 1940s; $5-7]

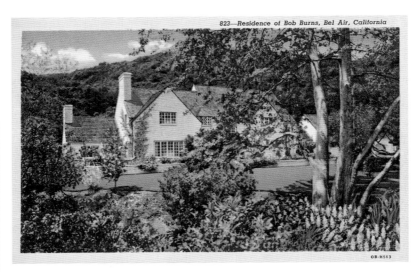

Home of Bob Burns, Van Buren, Arkansas. [c. 1940s; $3-5]

Bob Burns (1890-1956). Born in a small Arkansas town, Burns became known in film for his slow-talking country bumpkin character who always managed to outwit the city slickers. Prior to the big screen, he had a seventeen-year career in radio, first on Bing Crosby's *Kraft Music Hall* show and ultimately his own program from 1941 to 1947. He played bazooka and told tall tales about his mythical hillbilly relatives.

George Burns and Gracie Allen

855 Residence of Mr. and Mrs. George Burns (Gracie Allen), Beverly Hills, California

8A-H2993

Home of George Burns and Gracie Allen, Beverly Hills. [c. 1940s; $5-7]

George Burns (b.1896 - d.1996). George Burn's comedic career stretched from his youth in vaudeville, through radio, film, and television. Both were best-known for *The Burns & Allen Show* (on CBS and NBC from 1934 to 1950) in which Burns played straight man, Allen the scatterbrain. He was eighty years old when he won the 1976 Oscar for Best Supporting Actor for *The Sunshine Boys*, which was followed by another memorable performance in *Oh God* (1977).

Gracie Allen (b.1895 - d.1964). Born Ethel Cecile Roasalie Allen in San Francisco to show business parents, Allen was educated at a convent school before entering vaudeville herself. She married George Burns in 1929, and they adopted two children, Sondra and Ronnie. Allen was a private family person in real life, very unlike the scatterbrained woman she portrayed in her half of their show. She retired from film and television in the early 1940s.

Eddie Cantor

Home of Eddie Cantor, Beverly Hills. [c. 1940s; $5-7]

Home of Eddie Cantor, Beverly Hills. [c. 1950s; $5-7]

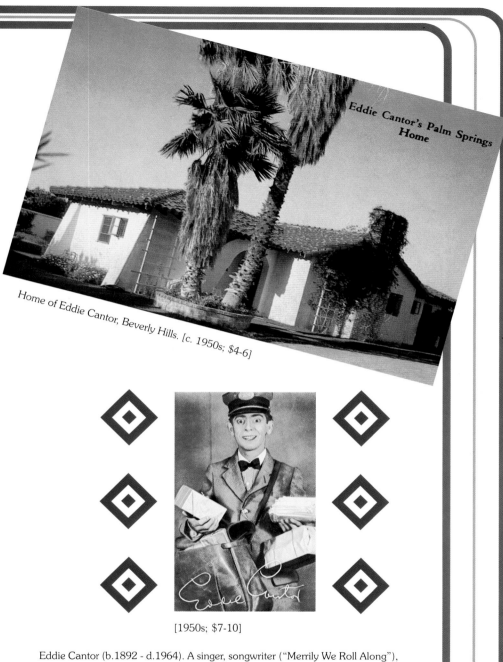

Home of Eddie Cantor, Beverly Hills. [c. 1950s; $4-6]

[1950s; $7-10]

Eddie Cantor (b.1892 - d.1964). A singer, songwriter ("Merrily We Roll Along"), comedian, author, and actor, Cantor entered show business in 1907 as a Vaudeville performer. He went on stage in Broadway productions, including *Banjo Eyes*, which earned him the same nickname, and the *Ziegfeld Follies* of 1917, 1918, 1919, and 1927. He had his own radio program in the 1930s, and was a television regular in the 1950s. His popular song compositions include *Get a Little Fun Out of Life* and *It's Great to Be Alive*. He also wrote books, and invented the name "March of Dimes" to combat polio.

Jeff Chandler

Home of Jeff Chandler, Palm Springs.
[c. 1950s; $5-7]

Jeff Chandler (b.1918 - d.1961). This heartthrob
had leading roles in more than thirty movies
between 1949 and 1962, and received an Oscar
nomination for his role in the movie *Broken Arrow*.
Born in Brooklyn, New York, he spent two years in
summer stock before serving in World War II. Radio
roles followed, then film in 1947. He became a top
leading man during the 1950s. Grey hair only
added to his sex appeal, but his maturing roles were
cut short when he died at the young age of forty-
two following spinal surgery.

1950s; $8-10

Charlie Chaplin

Charles Chaplin's California Home.

Home of Charles Chaplin, Hollywood. [c. 1930s; $5-7]

Home of Charlie Chaplin, Beverly Hills. [c. 1930s; $5-7]

Home of Charlie Chaplin, Beverly Hills. [c. 1940s; $5-7]

Charlie Chaplin Studio, Los Angeles. [c. 1930s; $6-8]

Charles Spencer Chaplin (b.1889 - d.1977). Born in London to stage parents, necessity drove Chaplin to work at age ten. He debuted with a juvenile group and distinguished himself as a tap dancer. He came to the United States in 1910 as a vaudeville comedian, and appeared before the cameras for the first time in 1913. He was an instant success in motion pictures. In 1917, Chaplin set out as an independent producer and busied himself with the construction of his own studios in the heart of the residential section of Hollywood at La Brea Avenue. In 1919, Chaplin joined forces with Mary Pickford, Douglas Fairbanks, and D.W. Griffith to found the United Artists Corporation.

Claudette Colbert

HOME OF CLAUDETTE COLBERT, HOLMBY HILLS, CALIFORNIA

T-359

62680

Home of Claudette Colbert, Holmby Hills. [c. 1940s; $5-7]

Claudette Colbert (b.1903 - d.1996). Her Broadway debut in 1923 led to a contract with Paramount. Her first big film success followed in 1932 when Cecil B. DeMille cast her as the wicked Poppea in *The Sign of the Cross* and DeMille brought out the haughty sensuality and earthy humor that finally set her apart. Subsequently, she earned an Oscar for Best Actress in *It Happened One Night* (1934), and played the femme fatale in *Cleopatra* (1934).

[c. 1930s; $10-12]

CLAUDETTE COLBERT

883 THE HILLTOP RESIDENCE OF CLAUDETTE COLBERT OVERLOOKS HOLLYWOOD, CALIFORNIA

PARAMOUNT STAR

3A-H1320

Home of Claudette Colbert, Hollywood. [c. 1940s; $5-7]

Betty Compson

Home of Betty
Compson,
Hollywood.
[c. 1930s;
$5-7]

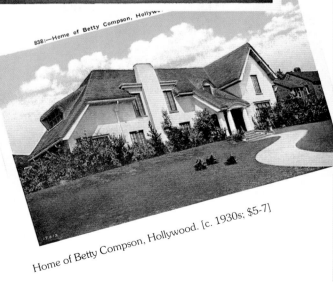

838:—Home of Betty Compson, Hollyw...

Home of Betty Compson, Hollywood. [c. 1930s; $5-7]

Betty Compson (b.1897 - d.1974). Born Eleanor Luicime Compson in Beaver, Utah, she enjoyed a prolific career, with twenty-five performances in 1916 alone. In 1928 she was nominated for the Academy Award for Best Actress for her role in *The Barker*. Her final film was *Here Comes Trouble* (1948), after which she retired to help her husband run his business, Ashtrays Unlimited.

Gary Cooper

782 HOME OF GARY COOPER, BRENTWOOD HEIGHTS, CALFORNIA

Home of Gary Cooper, Brentwood Heights.
[c. 1940s; $5-7]

Gary Cooper (b.1901 - d.1961). Born Frank James
Cooper, the son of British immigrants, he was raised
on a ranch in Montana before being sent back to
England for a more formal education. This upbringing
gave him the unique poise of a gentleman combined
with the rugged skills of a ranch hand. He entered film
work in 1926, after seeking work as a cowboy extra,
and learned his craft on the job. His first sound picture
was *The Virginian* (1929). His ability to portray both
gentleman and adventurers earned him a great variety
of roles, including his Oscar-winning part in *Sergeant
York* (1941) and a convincing baseball great Lou
Gehrig in *Pride of the Yankees* (1942). Too old to
serve, Cooper did dangerous entertainment detail in
the South Pacific during World War II. He was mostly
typecast in Westerns following the war, until his early
death from lung cancer.

MARLENE DIETRICH AND GARY COOPER

[c. 1940s; $8-10]

Joan Crawford

T116

Home of Joan Crawford, Brentwood Heights [c. 1940s; $5-7]

HOME OF JOAN CRAWFORD, BRENTWOOD HEIGHTS, CALIFORNIA

821   Residence of Joan Crawford, Brentwood, California

8A-H3005

Home of Joan Crawford, Brentwood Heights [c. 1940s; $5-7]

Home of Joan Crawford
Brentwood, Calif.
World Famous Motion Picture
Star

"Plastichrome" by *Colourpicture, Boston 15, Mass., U.S.A.*
DISTRIBUTED BY A. NITOCK & SONS, 13561 VENTURA BLVD., SHERMAN OAKS, CALIF.

ADDRESS ONLY

Home of Joan Crawford, Brentwood Heights [c. 1950s; $5-7]

[1930s; $15-20]

Joan Crawford (b.1908 - d.1977). Crawford made more than ninety films during a fifty-year career. Her Academy Award winning performance was in *Mildred Pierce* (1945) and two Oscar nominations for *Possessed* (1947) and *Sudden Fear* (1952). She went on to star in *Whatever Happened to Baby Jane?* in 1962 but had few favorable rolls after that. After 1974, Joan retired and devoted herself to the study of Christian Science. Joan Crawford died of pancreatic cancer in 1977.

Bing Crosby

Home of Bing Crosby, North Hollywood. [c. 1940s; $5-7]

Home of Bing Crosby, North Hollywood. [c. 1940s; $6-8]

Home of Bing Crosby, Palm Springs. [c. 1950s; $5-7]

Home of Bing Crosby, Palm Springs. [c. 1950s; $5-7]

BING CROSBY

PARAMOUNT

[1930s; $15]

47

[1950s; $10-12]

Bing Crosby (b.1904 - d.1977). Bing Crosby is one of the most successful recording artists of all time, with record sales estimated in the hundreds of millions of dollars worldwide. He recorded more than 1,700 songs, 368 of which made the charts; forty-two hit Number one including his biggest selling singles, "White Christmas" and "Silent Night." His star rose overnight in 1932 through a series of star radio appearances and a record breaking run on stage at New York's famed Paramount Theatre. His first film was The Big Broadcast of 1932. He won an Oscar for Best Actor for Going My Way (1944) and was nominated again for The Bells of St. Mary's (1945) and The Country Girl (1954). Four songs that he introduced in his films won Oscars, fourteen were nominated. His first television Christmas special aired in 1957 and it soon became an annual event lasting until his death.

Viola Dana

839:—Home of Viola Dana, Hollywood, Calif.

Home of Viola Dana, Hollywood.
[c. 1930s; $5-7]

Viola Dana (b.1897 - d.1987). Viola Dana began her career on Broadway as the lead in the original production of *Poor Little Rich Girl* (1913), which led to film. She married Edison Studio's top director, John H. Collins, and the two collaborated on several films before Collins died during the influenza epidemic of 1918. During the 1920s, she was one of Metro company's leading ladies until her fame began to wane in the late 1920s. Never a success in the "talkies," she worked in vaudeville before retiring as the wife of western star/stunt man "Lefty" Flynn.

[1930s; $10-12]

49

Marion Davies

Home of Marion Davies, Beverly Hills. [c. 1920s; $8-10]

Home of Marion Davies, Beverly Hills. [c. 1930s; $5-7]

HOME OF MARION DAVIES, BEVERLY HILLS, CALIF.   A82

RESIDENCE OF MARION DAVIES, BEVERLY HILLS, CALIFORNIA

Home of Marion Davies, Beverly Hills.
[c. 1930s; $5-7]

Home of Marion Davies, Santa Monica. [c. 1930s-40s; $5-7]

MARION DAVIES

Marion Davies (b.1897 - d.1961). Blonde and beautiful, Davies was first in demand as a model by the era's famous painters. She then made a name for herself on Broadway appearing in *Chin-Chin*, *Stop Look and Listen*, *Ziegfeld Follies*, and many other productions between 1915 and 1917. An alliance with publishing magnate William Randolph Hearst helped bolster her as "the most famously advertised actress in the world," and she appeared in forty-five films in the next two decades, averaging 2-3 per year. William Randolph Hearst built Davies a palatial beach house where she distinguished herself as a hostess. Dignitaries and celebrities from around the world were eager to accept her invitations, many of which were extended on behalf of the multiple charities she worked tirelessly for.

[1930s $10]

Bette Davis

Home of Bette Davis, North Hollywood. [c. 1940s; $6-8]

[1930s; $20]

[1950s; $10]

Bette Davis (b.1908 - d.1989). A star graduate of John Murray Anderson's Dramatic School, Davis's landed a Broadway debut in 1929, and a contract with Universal in 1930. She became a star after her appearance in *The Man Who Played God* and *Of Human Bondage*. She won the Best Actress Academy Award for *Dangerous* and *Jezebel*. In the 1940s, her films began to disappoint, though she made a huge comeback in 1950 for her Oscar-nominated role in *All About Eve*. Another Oscar nomination for her role as a demented former child star in *What Ever Happened to Baby Jane?* (1962) brought a new phase of stardom in both movies and television through the '60s and '70s. She received the AFI's Lifetime Achievement Award in 1977 and a Best Actress Emmy for *Strangers: The Story of a Mother and Daughter* (1970).

Dennis Day

Dennis Day's
Palm Springs Home

Home of Dennis Day, Palm Springs.
[c. 1950s; $5-7]

Dennis Day (b.1915 - d.1988). A career
widely contained to radio, tenor Dennis
Day is best known for his "teenage"
character on *The Jack Benny Program*
whose catch-phrase was an enthusiastic
"Gee, Mr. Benny." Day was voted one of
the five most popular radio tenors in
1939 which was also his first year on *The
Jack Benny Program*. He stayed with the
program until Benny's death in 1974.
Dennis never sang professionally after
that. He appeared in several films
between 1940 and 1976.

1940s; $10

Priscilla Dean

836:—Home of Priscilla Dean, Beverly Hills, Calif.

Home of Priscilla Dean, Beverly Hills. [c. 1930s; $5-7]

Pricilla Dean as Laura Figlan in *Reputation*. [c. 1930s; $10-12]

Priscilla Dean (1896 - d.1988). Born to theatrical parents, Dean was a seasoned professional by her tenth birthday. Her first film appearance was at age fourteen, and by 1911 she was landing lead roles in many comedies. By 1917, she had become very popular as the heroine of the *Gray Ghost* series, and maintained her popularity through the mid-'20s.

Jack Dempsey

731:—Jack Dempsey Home, Los Angeles, Calif.

Home of Jack Dempsey, Los Angeles. [c. 1930s; $5-7]

Jack Dempsey (1895 - d.1983). Rising from itinerant worker and barroom brawler, to world heavyweight champion, Dempsey dominated in the 1920s golden age of sports. Fans flocked to see him, helping him draw the first $1 million gate and the first $2 million gate. One of four wives, actress Estelle Taylor helped introduce him to the Hollywood life, and Dempsey starred in five movies and documentaries in the 1950s and '60s, primarily playing himself.

Elliot Dexter

Home of Elliot Dexter, Hollywood.
[c. 1930s; $5-7]

Elliot Dexter (b.1870 - d.1941). Elliot Dexter had logged many years with vaudeville and theater before moving into leading man roles in silent films at the ripe age of forty-five. A handsome man, he became typecast as the tuxedo-clad urbane hero in many Cecil B. DeMille productions.

[1930s; $10-12]

58

Walt Disney

Walt Disney's Palm Springs Home

Home of Walt Disney, Palm Springs. [c. 1950s; $5-7]

Walt Disney (b.1901 - d.1966). During his heyday, Disney was awarded twenty-nine Oscars for his films, and, by the 1960s, he had become the king of American entertainment. He is an icon of 20th century America, epitomizing the rise from humble beginnings toward infinite possibilities. He launched himself with beloved animated cartoon characters, starting with Oswald Rabbit and Mickey Mouse and the world's first feature-length animated film, *Snow White and the Seven Dwarfs* (1937), a project that grossed nearly $8 million.

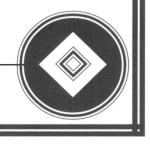

Kirk Douglas

Home of Kirk Douglas, Palm Springs. [c. 1950s; $5-7]

Kirk Douglas (b.1916 -). In addition to acting in countless films over the course of his long career, Douglas has served as a director and producer. He emerged as a full-fledged star with his portrayal of an ambitious boxer in *Champion* (1949), simultaneously typecasting himself as an intense, powerful, self-assured man and receiving his first Oscar nomination. More Oscar nominations followed for his work in *The Bad and the Beautiful* (1952) and *Lust for Life* (1956.) Other awards include the American Cinema Award (1987), the National Board of Review's Career Achievement Award (1989), an honorary Oscar by the Academy (1995), and the American Film Institute's Lifetime Achievement Award (1999). He has also written two novels: *Dance with the Devil* (1990) and *The Secret* (1992), and his autobiography, *The Ragman's Son.*

GREETINGS   Warner Bros.

KIRK DOUGLAS

[1940s; $10-12]

Irene Dunne

HOME OF IRENE DUNNE, HOLMBY HILLS, CALIFORNIA   T-364

Home of Irene Dunne, Holmby Hills [c. 1940s; $5-7]

817   HOME OF IRENE DUNNE

John Hughes Photo

Home of Irene Dunne, Holmby Hills [c. 1940s; $6-8]

IRENE DUNNE

[1930s; $10-12]

Irene Dunne (b.1898 - d.1990). Dunne's initial ambition was toward opera. However, she failed an audition with New York City's Metropolitan Opera and turned to musical comedy, debuting on Broadway in 1923. In 1929, she signed a movie contract with RKO and soon became one of the top dramatic stars at that studio. She retired from films in 1950, though she remained active in television, notably in Catholic-oriented programs, and became active in charitable work and conservative political causes.

Deanna Durbin

Home of Deanna Durbin, Hollywood. [c. 1940s; $6-8]

[1930s; $15-20]

[c. 1940s; $8-10]

Deanna Durbin (b.1921 -). This Canadian actress/singer was blessed at a very early age with a strong set of vocal chords. Universal cast her in a series of musicals, beginning in 1936 with *Three Smart Girls* that exploited her remarkable operatic voice while portraying her as a "regular kid." Durbin was awarded a 1938 special Oscar "for bringing to the screen the spirit and personification of youth." Her first screen kiss (from Robert Stack) in *First Love* (1939) made front-page news nationwide. Her box office draw waning, along with her own interest in filmmaking, she retired in 1948 into virtual anonymity.

Julian Eltinge

797:—Julian Eltinge's Home, Hollywood, Calif.

Home of Julian Eltinge, Hollywood.
[c. 1930s; $5-7]

Julian Eltinge (b.1882 - d.1941). Eltinge was vaudeville's most famous female imperson- ator. He appeared in drag for Boston revues as early as age ten. He had an uncanny ability to imitate feminine mannerisms and critics praised his excellent taste in dazzling gowns. He starred in Jerome Kern's Broadway musical *Mr. Wix of Wickham* (1904). He was in several films including *How Molly Made Good* (1915) in which he played himself, though his popularity didn't long outlast the demise of vaudeville.

[1920s-30s; $10-12]

65

Douglas Fairbanks

Home of Douglas Fairbanks, Sr. and Mary Pickford, Beverly Hills. [c. 1930s; $5-7]

793:—Home of Mary and Douglas Fairbanks, Beverly Hills, Calif.

804:—Private Swimming Pool and Home of "Doug. and Mary", Beverly Hills, California

Home of Douglas Fairbanks, Sr. and Mary Pickford [c. 1930s; $5-7]

850   MARY AND DOUG AT HOME "PICKFAIR", BEVERLY HILLS, CALIFORNIA

Home of Douglas Fairbanks, Sr. and Mary Pickford, Beverly Hills. [c. 1930s; $6-8]

106352

The Mary Pickford-Douglas Fairbanks Residence, Beverly Hills, California.

Home of Douglas Fairbanks, Sr. (b.1883 - d.1939) and Mary Pickford, Beverly Hills.1920s; $5-7

[1920s; $15-20]

DOUGLAS FAIRBANKS

[1920s; $15-20]

Douglas Fairbanks, Sr. (b.1883 - d.1939). Fairbanks came
to his love of theatrics via his Shakespearean-scholar
father, though he found the stage too confining. He entered
the motion picture industry in 1915 in *The Lamb*.
Fairbanks became the top moneymaker for the Triangle
Film Company, specializing in free-wheeling comedies. In
1920, Fairbanks starred in the swashbuckling *The Mark of
Zorro* (1920) and spent the remainder of his silent movie
career producing fast-paced, lavish costume epics. His
movies did not fare well in the talkie era. See Mary
Pickford, page 122.

Alice Faye and Phil Harris

846—Residence of Alice Faye, Beverly Hills, California

OB-H509

Home of Alice Faye, Beverly Hills. [c. 1940s; $6-8]

Alice Faye (b.1915 - d.1998). Alice Faye Leppert lied about her age at fourteen to land a chorus girl job. She became mistress to the show's star, Rudy Vallee, and he helped get her cast in her first film role *George White's Scandals* (1934). Successive films help establish her as a tough, contralto-voiced cookie with a heart of gold. Despite her rising popularity, she clashed with 20th Century Fox head man Darryl F. Zanuck, a feud that escalated to the point where Faye quit the movie industry. She flourished in radio, co-starring with her second husband, Phil Harris on a popular comedy series, which ran for several successful seasons.

[1930s; $10-12]

Home of Alice Faye and Phil Harris, Palm Springs. [c. 1950s; $4-6]

[1930s; $4-6]

Phil Harris (b.1904 - d.1995). Drummer/ bandleader Phil Harris made his screen debut in the RKO short "So This is Harris" (1933). He was a regular on *The Jack Benny Program* radio broadcasts of the 1930s and 1940s, his character a drinker and womanizer. On his own radio series, *The Phil Harris-Alice Faye Show* (1946-1954), he played the dim but good-natured husband, intellectually outclassed by his wife and two daughters. His hit songs began to incorporate children's tunes, and later he found work doing cartoon voiceovers for Disney feature films. The Broadway musical *The Music Man* was written for Harris, though he refused to appear in it or revival stagings.

71

Louise Fazenda

Home of Louise Fazenda, Los Angeles. [c. 1930s; $5-7]

Louise Fazenda (b.1895 - d.1962). Fazenda was a gifted character actress, with a comic gift and a willingness to do anything for a laugh. Typically, she portrayed unpolished country bumpkins ripe for seduction and abandonment. Following her starring role in *Down on the Farm* (1920), Fazenda experienced great popularity until her retirement in 1939. She remained active in charitable and humanitarian causes until her death.

Errol Flynn

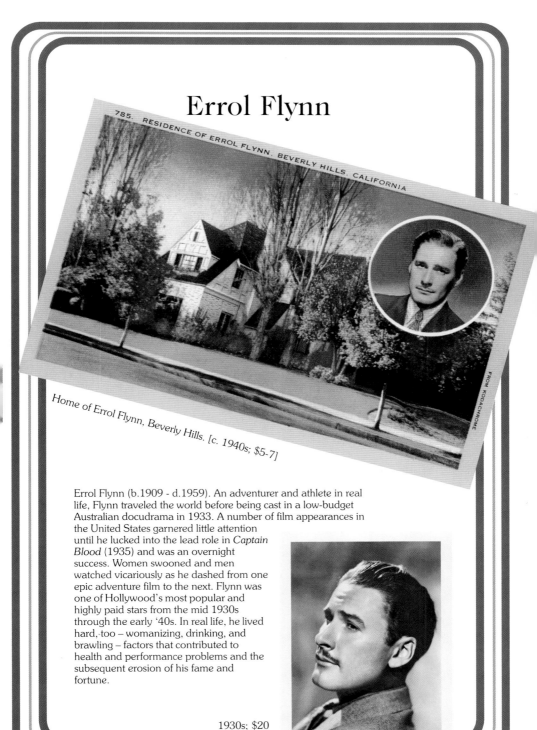

785. RESIDENCE OF ERROL FLYNN. BEVERLY HILLS, CALIFORNIA

FROM KODACHROME

Home of Errol Flynn, Beverly Hills. [c. 1940s; $5-7]

Errol Flynn (b.1909 - d.1959). An adventurer and athlete in real life, Flynn traveled the world before being cast in a low-budget Australian docudrama in 1933. A number of film appearances in the United States garnered little attention until he lucked into the lead role in *Captain Blood* (1935) and was an overnight success. Women swooned and men watched vicariously as he dashed from one epic adventure film to the next. Flynn was one of Hollywood's most popular and highly paid stars from the mid 1930s through the early '40s. In real life, he lived hard, too – womanizing, drinking, and brawling – factors that contributed to health and performance problems and the subsequent erosion of his fame and fortune.

1930s; $20

Errol Flynn

Pauline Frederick

Home of Pauline Frederick, Beverly Hills. [c. 1930s; $5-7]

805:—Pauline Frederick's Home, Beverly Hills, Calif.

RESIDENCE OF PAULINE FREDERICK, BEVERLY HILLS, CALIFORNIA

Home of Pauline
Frederick, Beverly Hills.
[c. 1930s; $5-7]

Pauline Frederick (b.1883 - d.1938). Getting her start as a chorus girl in the 1902 musical *The Rogers Brothers in Harvard*, she eventually established herself as one of Broadway's most versatile dramatic actresses. Her film debut in *Famous Players in Famous Play* (1915) proved her versatility, and she enjoyed popularity on screen throughout the 1920s. She landed a handful of choice character roles in talkies, including her final performance *Thank You, Mr. Moto* (1937).

Clarke Gable

795   HOME OF CLARK GABLE. BRENTWOOD HIGHLANDS. CALIF.

Home of Clarke Gable, Brentwood Highlands [c. 1940s; $6-8]

4A-H2095

Home of Clarke Gable, Brentwood Highlands [c. 1940s; $5-7]

Clarke Gable (b.1901 - d.1960). At sixteen, Gable saw his first stage play and was hooked. He left the oil fields on his twenty-first birthday to work in stock companies. His first wife, veteran actress Josephine Dillon coached him in speech and movement and paid to have his teeth fixed. Gable climbed his way up through regional theater, road shows, and movie extra roles. A Los Angeles stage production of *The Last Mile* (1930) caught the attention of film studios, and he began to land roles as villains and gangsters. He won an Oscar in *It Happened One Night* (1934). In 1939 he was cast as Rhett Butler in *Gone With the Wind*, garnering in the process the nickname "King of Hollywood." When his wife, Carole Lombard was killed in a tragic plane crash in 1942, Gable was left despondent. As a death wish, he enlisted in the Army Air Corps as a tail gunner. The move actually boosted his vitality and his popularity. That popularity, however, didn't shore up his ensuing movies, which were largely disappointing.

Home of Clarke Gable and Carole Lombard, Encino. [c. 1940s; $6-8]

814 Ranch Home of Clark Gable, Encino, California

65-H541

CLARK GABLE

METRO GOLDWYN · MAYER PICTURES

1930s; $20

814—Ranch Home of Clark Gable, Encino, California

IB-H1015

[c. 1940s; $6-8]

Carole Lombard (b.1908 - d.1942), Encino. Established as a bathing beauty in silent films, Lombard proved herself capable in comedy, drama, and satire, and received an Oscar nomination for *My Man Godfrey* (1936). Her last film was *To Be Or Not To Be.* Unfortunately, she died in a 1942 plane crash and did not live to see the film's premiere.

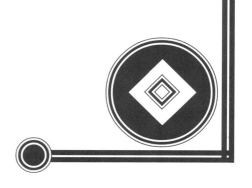

Judy Garland

Home of Judy Garland, Bel Air. [c. 1940s; $6-8]

848 — Residence of Judy Garland, Bel Air, California

OB-H506

FROM KODACHROME BY JUSMET

Home of Judy Garland, Bel Air. [c. 1940s; $6-8]

Judy Garland

[1940s; $15-20]

Judy Garland (b.1922 - d.1969). A performer since the age of two, Garland led an epic life of highs and lows, all avidly overseen by an adoring public. Born Frances Ethel Gumm, she toured the lesser circuits of vaudeville shows with her two sisters and parents for years, and appeared with her siblings in her first short film, *Starlet Revue/The Big Revue* (1929). She landed a contract with MGM in 1935, and was an emerging teen starlet when MGM awarded her the coveted role of Dorothy Gale in *The Wizard of Oz* (1939). Her rendition of "Over the Rainbow" won an Oscar. As her fame soared, Garland 's personal life unwound, with drug addictions and short-lived marriages and alliances that took a toll on her health. Nonetheless, she logged dozens of notable performances on screen and gave birth to daughter, Liza Minnelli. Late or ill-prepared for work time and again, MGM began replacing her in movies and finally dropped her in 1950. At age twenty-eight, with a young daughter and two failed marriages, Judy Garland's Hollywood career seemed at an end. She went on tour giving concerts under the guidance of Sid Luft, a manager who soon became husband number three, and father to daughter Lorna Luft. Together with Luft, they produced *A Star is Born* (1954), a film Garland called "the story of my life." It earned six Oscar nominations including Best Actress for Garland, and one for the song "The Man That Got Away." It did not, however, revive her film career. She entered the relatively new realm of television with her own variety series *The Judy Garland Show* (CBS, 1963-64). When the show was canceled, Garland was in debt and essentially homeless. She continued to perform live until just before her death of an accidental overdose of prescription drugs.

80

Cary Grant

Home of Cary Grant, Palm Springs. [c. 1950s; $5-7]

Cary Grant (b.1904 - d.1986). Grant embodied the iconic, slick, dashing image that personifies "Hollywood Star." Born impoverished in England, and named Archibald Alexander Leach, the young boy began working odd jobs at a music hall when he was nine. He joined a comedy troupe at fourteen, performing dance, acrobatic stunts, stilt-walking, and pantomime throughout England. He sailed to the United States in 1920 for a two-year tour, after which Grant stuck around and picked up odd jobs in New York until he landed his first stage part in 1927. His first film followed in 1931, in a ten-minute short, after which he moved to California and adopted his new name. Two films, *Topper* and *The Awful Truth* (both 1937) launched his star, and a succession of hits followed, each of which honed his big-screen idol image, climaxing with *The Philadelphia Story* (1940). Future film efforts were largely unsuccessful, with the exception of a few Alfred Hitchcock roles. In 1966, Grant retired from film.

[1940s; $15-20]

John Gilbert

871 JOHN GILBERT'S SPANISH HOME IN BEVERLY HILLS, CALIFORNIA

121861

Home of John Gilbert, Beverly Hills. [c. 1930s; $5-7]

John Gilbert (b.1899 - d.1936). The son of itinerant actors, Gilbert's brooding good looks made him a superstar of the silent film era, headlining dozens of box-office hits. In addition to romantic alliances with top starlets, including Greta Garbo and Marlene Dietrich, Gilbert experienced stormy relationships with studio executives. These quarrelsome relationships, and heavy drinking, were more likely the cause of his downfall when the talkie era got underway. He was cast in a series of ill-fated films before dying young and suddenly of a heart attack.

JOHN GILBERT

[1930s; $10-12]

82

HOME OF JOHN GILBERT, BEVERLY HILLS, CALIF.

A84

Home of John Gilbert, Beverly Hills. [c. 1930s; $5-7]

Corinne Griffith

Home of Corinne Griffith, Beverly Hills. [c. 1930s; $5-7]

Home of Corinne Griffith, Beverly Hills. [c. 1930s; $5-7]

814A:—Corinne Griffith's Home, Beverly Hills, Calif.

Home of Corinne Griffith, Beverly Hills. [c. 1930s; $5-7]

Corinne Griffith (b.1894 - d.1979). Launched by a beauty contest win, Griffith signed a film contract in 1916, and had worked her way up to leading lady by the following year. Her greatest hit was *The Divine Lady* (1927). She tried a few talkies, then left film and tried stage in the early 1930s. A second career in real estate and the stock market made her one of the wealthiest women in the world. She also went on to write several books, one of which was made into a movie, *Papa's Delicate Condition* (1963).

Ann Harding

812 ANN HARDING'S HILLTOP HOME, HOLLYWOOD, CALIFORNIA

2A-H32

Home of Ann Harding, Hollywood. [c. 1940s; $5-7]

Ann Harding (b.1901 - d.1981). Born Dorothy Walton Gatley, she was raised in a military family and frequently relocated throughout the United States during her childhood. She went on stage at the age of twenty and, rising from Broadway roles, Harding fell into the leading role of self-sacrificing heroine in a number of mid-1930s films. She received an Oscar nomination for *Holiday* (1930). She retired in 1937 when she married Werner Janssen, a symphony conductor. In 1942, she returned for intermittent screen work, primarily in maternal roles.

[1930s; $20]

ANN HARDING   RADIO PICTURES

William S. Hart

811:—Wm. S. Hart's Home, Hollywood, California

RESIDENCE OF WM. HART,
HOLLYWOOD,
LOS ANGELES, CALIFORNIA

Homes of William S. Hart, Hollywood. [c. 1930s; $5-7 each]

1930s; $10-12

William S. Hart (b.1870 - d.1946). A stage actor in New York at age nineteen, by his thirty's Hart had grown from Shakespearean actor to his favorite roles, Western plays. He began film work in 1914, at the age of forty-four. Playing first villains, then heroes, he rose to rank among the top three male stars between 1910-1912. Drawing on his memories of the West when he was the son of an itinerate worker, he began writing and directing his own films, creating stark sets and storylines that emphasized plot and character over glamour. In the early '20s the public's taste swung toward spectacular action movies and Hart's popularity faded. He retired to write western novels along with his autobiography, *My Life: East and West* (1929).

WILLIAM S. HART
As Ovit Miller in "White Oak."
A Paramount Picture, Directed by Lambert Hillyer

Sessue Hayakawa

796:—Home of Sessue Hayakawa, Hollywood, California

Home of Sessue Hayakawa, Hollywood. [c. 1930s; $5-7]

Sessue Hayakawa (b.1888 - d.1951). One of the first Japanese actors to make it in Hollywood, he first came to the United States with an acting troupe. He was discovered by a producer, and wowed audiences with his subtlety on the silent screen. The following year, *The Typhoon* (1915) made him a star, and many roles followed. Generally, he was cast as a villain. His popularity waned by 1923, and Hayakawa moved to Europe to appear in films there. He returned to Hollywood in the late 1940s, and is remembered for his Oscar-nominated role in *The Bridge on the River Kwai* (1957).

[1930s; $10-12]

Jack Holt

800:—Home of Jack Holt, Hollywood, Calif.

Home of Jack Holt, Hollywood. [c. 1930s; $5-7]

Jack Holt (b.1888 - d.1951). A popular, virile he-man action hero of the 1920s, Holt was a hot ticket in the early talkie era. Comic strip artist Chester Gould admitted that his character, Dick Tracy, was drawn from Holt's likeness. Holt's popularity died with a series of poor films, and he did work as a supporting actor for the remainder of his life.

Bob Hope

816—Residence of Bob Hope, North Hollywood, California

Star of NBC and Motion Pictures

Home of Bob Hope, North Hollywood. [c. 1940s; $6-8]

Bob Hope (b.1903 - d. 2003). British born, Bob Hope became an American institution, offering "100 Years of Hope and Humor," the aptly-titled tribute television special staged in his honor during the last year of his life. Hope's beneficence toward American troops overseas was legendary, he traveled worldwide for live performances with star-studded variety shows from World War II theaters to the Persian Gulf War. Hope got his start as a shoe salesman at age sixteen, and would pick up change singing at local restaurants and saloons in Cleveland. Hope took up vaudeville full-time as young adult and soon found his niche in comedy. He failed his first screen test in 1929, but continued to rise in Vaudeville and radio. A choice role in a Broadway musical, *Roberta* (1933) led to a long run and the next gig was a comedy sketch with the *Ziegfeld Follies*, and playing alongside Ethel Merman and Jimmy Durante in *Red, Hot and Blue*. In 1937, a duet with Shirley Ross, "Thanks for the Memory" in *The Big Broadcast* of 1938 won him an Oscar and launched his movie career. Dozens of films, songs, and popular television specials followed for a résumé pages long.

Bob Hope's Palm Springs Home

Home of Bob Hope, Palm Springs. [c. 1950s; $5-7]

1930s; $15-20

Bob Hope
in dem Paramount-Farbfilm „Herz in der Hose"

Foto: Paramount

Reproduktion verboten

Jose Iturbi

820   HOME OF JOSE ITURBI

Home of Jose Iturbi. [c. 1940s; $6-8]

Jose Iturbi (b.1895 - d.1980). Of Basque descent, pianist Jose Iturbi was playing Spanish cabarets by the age of twelve. As a young adult, he supported himself as a silent-movie accompanist. His training and accomplishments were reflected in a post as head of the music department of the Conservatory of Geneva from 1919 to 1923, and eight years conducting the Rochester Philharmonic. Though he achieved pop-chart success with Spanish flavored compositions, Iturbi sought to spread the popularity of Classic music. He appeared in several MGM films, including *Three Daring Daughters* (1948).

Emil Jannings

Home of Emil Jannings, Hollywood. [c. 1930s; $6-8]

Emil Jannings (b.1884 - d.1950). In the mid 1920s, Jannings had an international reputation as the world's greatest screen actor. German born, he was disillusioned by work as a sailor and ocean liner cook, and joined the theater at age eighteen. In 1906, he joined Max Reinhardt's Berlin Theater, then considered the world's finest stage troupe. By 1919 he began appearing in a string of Germanic-slanted historical screen dramas, and by the mid 1920s had an international reputation as the world's greatest screen actor. Paramount signed him in 1927, bringing him to Hollywood to star in a number of films. Because of his thick German accent, the advent of sound ended his American career. Back in Germany, he was an avid Nazi supporter and propagandist, honored as "Artist of the State" in 1941. After the war, the Allied authorities blacklisted him and he never made another film.

Van Johnson

Home of Van Johnson, Beverly Hills. [c. 1950s; $5-7]

Van Johnson (b.1916 -). Working his way up from chorus boy on Broadway, to understudy, to B motion pictures, Johnson enjoyed a steady climb of sponsorship. Ironically, serious injuries suffered in a car accident proved a blessing when he failed to make the draft and subsequently found the doors wide open for young leading-men roles. The freckle-faced blonde became a hit with teen girls in *The Human Comedy* (1943), *A Guy Named Joe* (1943), and *Thirty Seconds Over Tokyo* (1944). His popularity continued though the 1950s, alternating serious characterizations with lightweight romantic fare. He juggled stage, screen, and some television work through the nineties, always managing to bring star quality to his roles. His 1976 work in *Rich Man, Poor Man* earned him an Emmy nomination, and recent work included televisions *Clowning Around* (1992).

[1940s; $10-12]

94

Buster Keaton

Home of Buster Keaton, Beverly Hills. [c. 1930s; $5-7]

Home of Buster Keaton, Beverly Hills. [c. 1930s; $5-7]

Buster Keaton

441/2   „Iris" Verlag

[1930s; $15-20]

Buster Keaton (b.1895 - d.1966). Considered one of the most gifted comedians of the silent film era, Keaton spent his entire life in show business. He began performing at age three in his parents vaudeville act. A fellow vaudeville comedian, Roscoe "Fatty" Arbuckle was starring in a low-budget two-reel screen comedy, *The Butcher Boy*, and invited Keaton to play a small role in the picture. The two began starring in a long string of comic screen hits. Keaton soon began writing and directing their pictures, and started starring in his own films as well. He delighted in the medium of film, playfully inventing special effects. Keaton "The Great Stone Face" developed a trademark deadpan demeanor merged with slapstick gags. He became a major star, and moved up to feature-length comedies in 1923, culminating in *The General*, now universally regarded as his masterpiece. Keaton's work suffered after he signed a contract with MGM, and his personal life did as well as he began to drink heavily, to the point where he had to be committed to a sanitarium. Stage parts and overseas films sustained him for years, until a now-sober Keaton started a comeback in 1949 with supporting roles in major movies. In the 1960s he was back in demand, appearing in American International Pictures' "Beach" Musicals and a number of TV ads.

Warren Kerrigan

827:—Warren Kerrigan's Home, Hollywood, Calif.

Home of J. Warren Kerrigan, Hollywood. [c. 1930s; $5-7]

[1920s; $12-15]

J. WARREN KERRIGAN
UNIVERSAL

Residence of J. Warren Kerrigan, Hollywood, Calif.

Home of J. Warren Kerrigan, Hollywood. [c. 1930s; $5-7]

J. Warren Kerrigan (b.1879 - d.1947). A star on stage as a juvenile, Kerrigan made his film debut in 1909 and within five years was America's most popular screen actor. He headlined hundreds of one and two-reel Westerns and outdoor melodramas. He won enormous public disfavor with his refusal to serve in World War I, citing his need to be with his ailing mother. A role in the smash hit *The Covered Wagon* (1923) revived his career momentarily.

Kay Kyser

2—The Home of Kay Kyser, Rocky Mount, N. C.

Home of Kay Kyser, Rocky Mount, North Carolina. [c. 1940s; $5-7]

Kay Kyser (b.1897 - d.1985). Kay Kyser studied drama at the University of North Carolina at Chapel Hill, working his way through school by leading a student band and, later, a hotel orchestra. In radio, he hit the big time in 1938 with the weekly NBC musical quiz program *Kay Kyser's Kollege of Musical Knowledge*. He helped bankroll his first starring film, *That's Right, You're Wrong* (1939), a huge hit that spawned a series of popular Kyser vehicles. He moved his radio show to TV in 1949, having vowed to retire from show business when he'd saved a million dollars; he did so in 1950.

Alan Ladd

Home of Alan Ladd, Palm Springs. [c. 1950s; $5-7]

Alan Ladd (b.1913 - d.1964). Ladd entered film work through bit parts as a mere teenager and landed a number of minor roles before agent, and future wife, Sue Carol "discovered him." A major role in *This Gun for Hire* (1942) launched him as a star, with many action adventure leads that captured his good looks. His most noteworthy work was in *Shane* (1953). Ladd fathered actors Alan Ladd Jr. and David Ladd, and former child actress Alana Ladd.

Alan Ladd's Palm Springs Home

Home of Alan Ladd, Palm Springs. [c. 1950s; $5-7]

[1950s; $8-10]

Carl Laemmle

CARL LAEMMLE'S HOME, BEVERLY HILLS, CALIFORNIA

T 132

Home of Carl Laemmle, Beverly Hills. [c. 1930s-40s; $5-7]

Carl Laemmle (b.1867 - d.1939). Enormously influential, Laemmle founded Universal Studios and was the original movie mogul. Rising from odd jobs in Chicago, he saved his pennies and invested in nickelodeons. This led to film distribution, and finally production and publicity. He added sizzle and hype to the "Biograph Girl," Florence Lawrence, and the next "America's Sweetheart" Mary Pickford. Laemmle played up their glamour, inundating the news with their exploits and publicly using their names at every opportunity. In this way, Laemmle began the star system that continues today. Buying up smaller companies he created the Universal Film Manufacturing Company, launching it at a new 230-acre facility called Universal City in 1915 with a huge public ceremony attended by over 20,000 fans.

Dorothy Lamour

786. RESIDENCE OF DOROTHY LAMOUR, BEVERLY HILLS, CALIFORNIA.

834—Residence of Dorothy Lamour, Beverly Hills, California

Home of Dorothy Lamour, Beverly Hills. [c. 1940s; $6-8]

[1940s; $6-8]

Dorothy Lamour (b.1914 - d.1996). A business degree and subsequent years spent tending an elevator in her hometown of New Orleans didn't satisfy Lamour. She joined a vaudeville troupe in 1930, and the following year landed work as a vocalist with a band. Prior to her film career, she built a solid reputation as a radio singer. In 1936, Paramount Studios signed her, creating an exotic south seas persona for her in *Jungle Princes* (1936) and ensuing successful "jungle" films. She was a major star by 1939. Beginning in 1940, she co-starred with Bob Hope and Bing Crosby in a series of six "Road" films that marked both the summit of her career, and the descent down the other side. Lamour was very popular with the World War II troops and toured extensively. She devoted time to her family between 1952 and 1962, and returned to limited stage, film, and television work in the 1960s and 1970s.

[1930s-40s; $15-20]

Liberace

Home of Liberace, Palm Springs. [c. 1950s; $5-7]

Home of Liberace, Sherman Oaks. [c. 1950s; $5-7]

[1930s; $15-20]

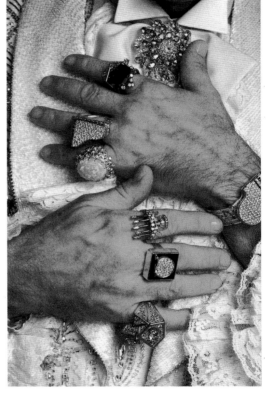

[1980s; $3-5]

Wladziu Valentino Liberace (b.1919 - d.1987). Raised in a musical family (his father played French horn in John Philip Sousa's Concert Band and the Milwaukee Symphony Orchestra), Liberace proved both child prodigy and eager performer. His merits on piano were enough to sustain him, but in the early 1950s he achieved star status among middle-aged and older female fan base. He set himself apart with his showy style and flamboyant costumes, and though a movie career failed at the start with *Sincerely Yours* (1955) he was a regular on television variety shows, and a favorite on the stages of Las Vegas.

Harold Lloyd

Home of Harold Lloyd, Beverly Hills. [c. 1930s; $5-7]

HOME OF HAROLD LLOYD, HOLLYWOOD, CALIFORNIA

Home of Harold Lloyd, Beverly Hills. [c. 1950s; $4-6]

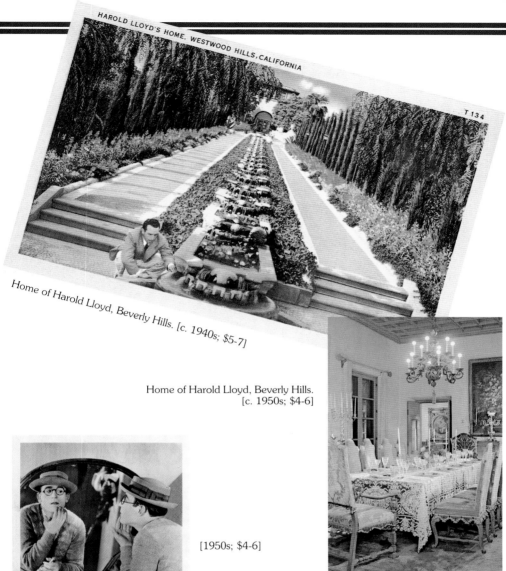

Home of Harold Lloyd, Beverly Hills. [c. 1940s; $5-7]

Home of Harold Lloyd, Beverly Hills.
[c. 1950s; $4-6]

[1950s; $4-6]

Harold Lloyd

Harold Lloyd (b.1894 - d.1971). As impossible as it seems, Lloyd created an average nice-guy character who was funny at all times. An average all-American all his life, Lloyd worked his way through odd jobs in the theater and with silent film companies. Film producer and friend Hal Roach and Lloyd both claimed credit for coming up with the "glasses" character – a handsome, normal looking youth who wore horned-rimmed glasses. In either case, the character was a huge hit and soon graduated from two-reelers to feature-length film. Lloyd formed his own production company in 1924, and his annual feature releases established him as the top moneymaking comedian in the movies. Lloyd's screen character didn't survive the Depression, and he left films as an actor in 1938. He was considered one the nicest, most accessible, and richest stars in Hollywood. He devoted the remainder of his life to his home, Greenacres, his wife Mildred Davis, their children, and his hobbies of painting and photography.

107

Myrna Loy

112:—HOME OF MYRNA LOY, HIDDEN VALLEY, BEVERLY HILLS, CALIFORNIA.

Home of Myrna Loy,
Beverly Hills. [c. 1940s;
$5-7]

Home of Myrna
Loy, Beverly Hills.
[c. 1940s; $6-8]

Myrna Loy (b.1905 - d.1993). Myrna Loy was known as
the Queen of Hollywood during the 1930s. Getting her start
as a dancer, she moved into silent films and smoothly
transitioned to talkies. Her bright, witty ideal wife persona
was established in 1934 with *The Thin Man* series, opposite
William Powell, and during the next two decades she
continued to play strong women roles including parts in
Libeled Lady (1936), *Wife vs. Secretary* (1936), and *Too
Hot to Handle* (1938). She worked with the Red Cross
during WWII and was active in politics later in life. She
received an honorary Oscar in 1991.

[1940s; $8-10]

108

Jayne Mansfield

Home of Jayne Mansfield, Beverly Hills. [c. 1950s; $8-10]

Jayne Mansfield (b.1933 - d.1967). At age sixteen, Vera Jane Palmer married student Paul James Mansfield and, unable to afford day-care, attended acting classes in Los Angeles carrying her infant daughter. Measuring 40-21-35, Mansfield was forever typecast as a Marilyn Monroe parody in television and film work, and earned the distinction of becoming the first major film starlet to appear nude on screen. Her roles were, for the most part, modest fare with the exception of *The Girl Can't Help It* (1956) and *Will Success Spoil Rock Hunter?* (1957). Her flair for publicity exploits are legendary. She died in a car accident in 1967.

[1950s; $15-20]

Frederick March

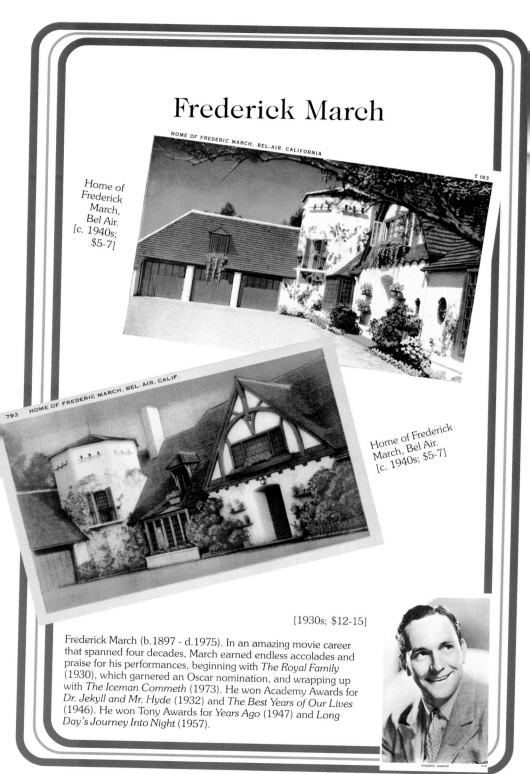

HOME OF FREDERIC MARCH, BEL-AIR, CALIFORNIA

T 193

Home of
Frederick
March,
Bel Air.
[c. 1940s;
$5-7]

793 HOME OF FREDERIC MARCH, BEL-AIR, CALIF.

Home of Frederick
March, Bel Air.
[c. 1940s; $5-7]

[1930s; $12-15]

Frederick March (b.1897 - d.1975). In an amazing movie career that spanned four decades, March earned endless accolades and praise for his performances, beginning with *The Royal Family* (1930), which garnered an Oscar nomination, and wrapping up with *The Iceman Commeth* (1973). He won Academy Awards for *Dr. Jekyll and Mr. Hyde* (1932) and *The Best Years of Our Lives* (1946). He won Tony Awards for *Years Ago* (1947) and *Long Day's Journey Into Night* (1957).

FREDRIC MARCH

Dean Martin

DEAN MARTIN'S
Palm Springs Home

Home of Dean Martin, Palm Springs. [c. 1950s; $5-7]

Dean Martin (b.1917 - d.1995). Successful in almost every entertainment venue, Martin first made his name as the straight-man in a comedy duo with Jerry Lewis in 1946, a partnership that weathered sixteen films. When that decade-long gig broke up, he recorded popular hits such as "That's Amore," "Volare," and "Everybody Loves Somebody Sometime" – recording more than 100 albums and over 500 songs. *The Dean Martin Show* (1965-1974) enjoyed a tremendous run on television, a variety show that cast Dean as a carefree boozer and womanizer. He became associated with Hollywood's hip "Rat Pack" and chief deputy to the "Chairman of the Board" Frank Sinatra. He was one of the most popular nightclub acts in Las Vegas for three decades.

[1950s; $10-12]

Groucho Marx

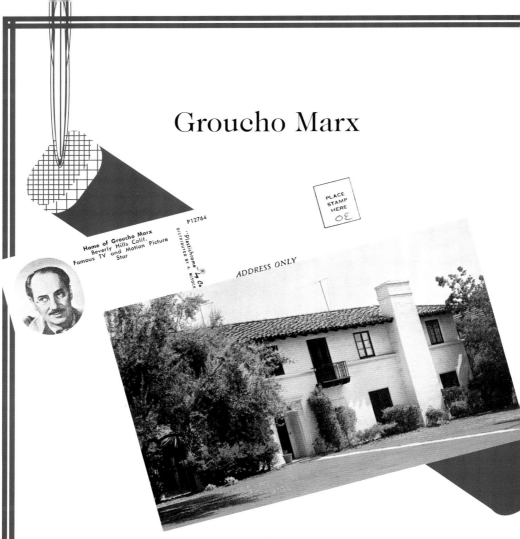

Home of Groucho Marx, Beverly Hills. [c. 1950s; $5-7]

Groucho Marx (b.1895 - d.1977). Starting out in an act organized by stage mother Minnie Marx, Groucho performed with his younger brother Gummo, sister Mabel, and brothers Chico and Harpo in a vaudeville act. The audience ate up his ad-lib wisecracks, and the four Marx Brothers metamorphosed into a comedy team. The Marx Brothers eventually accepted work with a Broadway-bound show, *I'll Say She Is* (1924). *The Cocoanuts* (1925) and *Animal Crackers* (1928) followed, and both were made into early talkies, launching the brothers into Hollywood and a series of screen comedies that stretched through 1941. Unsuccessful films and marginal radio appearances filled the gap until he was approached in 1947 to host a radio quiz show called *You Bet Your Life*. Groucho accepted on condition that he could be himself, ad-libbing to his heart's content with the contestants. *You Bet Your Life* was a rousing success on both radio (1947-1956) and television (1950-1961 on NBC), winning high ratings and several Emmys. In the early 1970s, his old films were rediscovered and he returned to active performing with TV guest appearances and a 1972 sold-out appearance at Carnegie Hall. In 1974 Marx accepted a special Oscar.

Cecil B. DeMille

817A:—Cecil B. De Mille's Home, Hollywood, Calif.

Home of Cecil B. DeMille, Hollywood. [c. 1930s; $5-7]

Cecil B. DeMille (b.1881 - d.1959). Raised in the theater, DeMille formed a partnership with two other men to produce films in his mid-twenties, co-writing, producing, and directing *The Squaw Man* (1914), an elaborate six-reel film that met with great success. This launched his highly lauded career as a director and filmmaker. DeMille took a hand in everything from editing and writing (or co-writing) almost all of his films, helping to develop the classic Hollywood narrative style. In addition to his contributions to how films were made in the early days, DeMille continued with a long career that helped illustrate the potential of big budget films translated into box-office blockbusters, as in his swan song, the spectacular *The Ten Commandments* (1956).

Tom Mix

Home of Tom Mix, Hollywood. [c. 1930s; $5-7]

HOME OF TOM MIX, HOLLYWOOD, CALIFORNIA

A-65

Tom Mix (b.1880 - d.1940). Tom Mix was an actual champion rodeo rider and Texas Ranger who went on to superstardom on the Hollywood set. His flashy, colorful screen character won over audiences in dozens of westerns, stretching from his first small role in 1910 through blockbuster Zane Grey adaptations including *The Lone Star Ranger* (1923) and *Riders of the Purple Sage* (1925). When the popularity of Westerns flagged, Mix took to the road in the late 1920s and '30s, touring with circuses, including the Tom Mix Circus.

A81

Home of Tom Mix, Beverly Hills. [c. 1930s; $5-7]

Marilyn Monroe

Home of Marilyn Monroe,
Beverly Hills. [c. 1950s; $8-10]

Marilyn Monroe (b.1926 - d.1962). This mythologized megastar was born Norma Jean Mortensen, and spent her childhood in an endless succession of orphanages and foster homes. Married as a young teen, divorced at age twenty, she bleached her hair and tried modeling and soon began appearing in national publications where she was "discovered" and signed with 20th Century Fox. Neither Fox nor Columbia produced significant roles, and her career languished until she landed a lead role in *Clash by Night* (1952), followed by publication of nude photos she had posed for two years earlier. Hits followed in quick succession in the mid 1950s, including light comedies that proved her strong suit, such as *Gentlemen Prefer Blondes* and *How to Marry a Millionaire*. Marriage to baseball legend Jo DiMaggio and a greatly publicized appearance for troops in Korea kept her in the headlines. She next started appearing in the news by boycotting her dumb blonde roles, and set out to better her skills at the Actors Studio in New York. There she met playwright Arthur Miller, whom she married. She struck a better deal with Fox that allowed her to hand-pick her projects, including *Bus Stop* (1956) and *Some Like it Hot* (1959). However, her reliance on drugs and alcohol became increasingly severe, her marriage to Miller crumbled, and she was fired early from her final film project and slapped with a lawsuit. A little more than a month later, Monroe died, officially due to an overdose of barbiturates. Yet conspiracy theories surrounding her death flourish just as her legend continues to grow.

[c. 1950s; $6-8]

Robert Montgomery

4A-H2094

Home of Robert Montgomery, Beverly Hills. [c. 1940s; $5-7]

Robert Montgomery (b.1904 - d.1981). Appearing in almost forty sound films, Montgomery distinguished himself as a light comedian and dramatic actor. He was nominated for an Academy Award for *Night Must Fall* (1937). However, his career took a more serious turn after he returned from military duty in World War II. He moved more into a directorial role, and his attentions turned to politics. He was a "friendly" witness at the infamous House Un-American Activities Committee hearings, which led to the Hollywood Backlist. In the mid 1950s he became a prestigious television producer. His anthology series *Robert Montgomery Presents* (1950-1957) won him an Emmy Award, and launched his daughter, Elizabeth, on her acting career. He also ventured on stage, winning a Tony Award for directing *The Desperate Hours* (1955).

1930s; $8-10

Colleen Moore

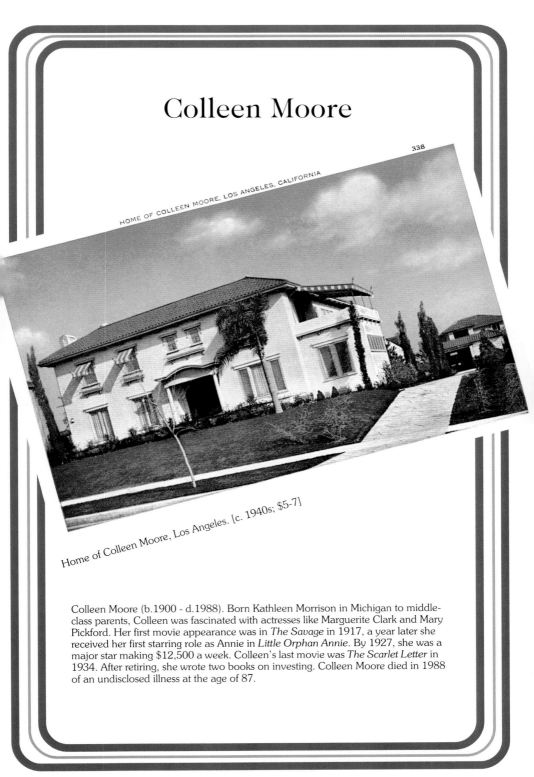

HOME OF COLLEEN MOORE, LOS ANGELES, CALIFORNIA

338

Home of Colleen Moore, Los Angeles. [c. 1940s; $5-7]

Colleen Moore (b.1900 - d.1988). Born Kathleen Morrison in Michigan to middle-class parents, Colleen was fascinated with actresses like Marguerite Clark and Mary Pickford. Her first movie appearance was in *The Savage* in 1917, a year later she received her first starring role as Annie in *Little Orphan Annie*. By 1927, she was a major star making $12,500 a week. Colleen's last movie was *The Scarlet Letter* in 1934. After retiring, she wrote two books on investing. Colleen Moore died in 1988 of an undisclosed illness at the age of 87.

Conrad Nagel

RESIDENCE OF CONRAD NAGEL,
BEVERLY HILLS, CALIFORNIA

Home of Conrad Nagel,
Beverly Hills. [c. 1930s; $5-7]

[1930s; $15-20]

CONRAD NAGEL
as John Shand in
"What Every Woman Knows"
in
A William De Mille-Paramount
Picture

Conrad Nagel (b.1897 - d.1970). One of the top screen idols of the silent age, Nagel
made an impressive debut in one of the first talkies, as well. His film career continued
until the 1940s, when he went on to work in radio, Broadway, and television. He was co-
founder of the Academy of Motion Picture Arts, serving for a time as its president and
helping to create the Academy Awards. He was awarded a special Oscar in 1947 for his
work on the Motion Picture Relief Fund, and was president of the Associated Actors and
Artists of American until his death.

Alla Nazimova

787:—Nazimova Residence, Los Angeles, California

Home of Alla Nazimova, Los Angeles. ·
[c. 1930s; $5-7]

Alla Nazimova (b.1879 - d.1945). An acclaimed
actress and violinist from Russia, Nazimova emigrated
to the United States in 1905 to work first on Broadway,
where she helped interpret Ibsen's work. In 1916 she
made her screen debut and went on to star in
numerous Hollywood films. She resumed her stage
career in 1925, and returned to film in character roles
in the early 1940s.

[1920s; $15-20]

MADAME NAZIMOVA
IN
REPERTOIRE

Pola Negri

[1930s; $6-8 each]

Home of Pola Negri, Beverly Hills. [c. 1930s; $5-7]

Pola Negri (b.1897 - d.1987). Born Appolonia Chalupek in Warsaw, Poland, Negri studied dance and performed in lead roles with the Imperial Ballet before tuberculosis struck her down. Upon her recovery, she enrolled at the Imperial Academy of Dramatic Arts in Warsaw and debuted as a stage and film actress in 1913. She became internationally famous in a number of major German films before Paramount lured and imported her as Hollywood's first imported star in 1923. Her running feud with Gloria Swanson garnered her a lot of publicity, along with an engagement to Charlie Chaplin which ended in a romantic alliance with Rudolph Valentino. She returned to Europe following the advent of talkies, married and divorced a Russian prince, and fought rumors that she was romantically involved with Hitler. In 1951, she became a U.S. citizen and authored an autobiography, *Pola Negri: Memoirs of a Star*.

120

Ozzie and Harriet Nelson

819 HOME OF THE NELSONS (OZZIE AND HARRIET)

John Hughes Photo

Home of Ozzie and Harriet Nelson. [c. 1940s; $6-8]

Harriet Nelson (b.1909 - d.1994). Born to actors, Harriet Hilliard first made her mark as a vaudeville and nightclub singer. She made a film with Fred Astaire and Ginger Rogers, *Follow the Fleet*, in 1936, but her career path continued in clubs and then radio as the vocalist for the Ozzie Nelson Orchestra. She married Nelson in 1935, and changed her name. They launched their popular radio sitcom, *The Adventures of Ozzie and Harriet*, in 1944, moving to television (1952-1966) and adding their real-life sons David and Ricky to the act.

Ozzie Nelson (b.1906 - d.1975). Operating a dance band was a hobby while Nelson studied law, but it proved quite profitable and eventually won all his focus. Nelson's band played prestigious East Coast venues like the Glen Island Casino and the New Yorker Hotel. His relaxed, singing style proved remarkably popular, as did his romantic duets with Harriet Hilliard. After their marriage and the launch of their radio-to-television show, the Nelsons grew to epitomize the ideal, all-American family of the 1950s.

1940s; $12-18.

Mary Pickford

Home of Mary Pickford, Beverly Hills [c. 1930s; $5-7]

THE RESIDENCE OF MARY PICKFORD, BEVERLY HILLS, CALIFORNIA

850—Residence of Mary Pickford, Beverly Hills, California

3A-H1073

Home of Mary Pickford, Beverly Hills. [c. 1940s; $5-7]

Mary Pickford (b.1892 - d.1979). Pickford was truly Hollywood's first true superstar. Billed as "America's Sweetheart," she was the greatest screen icon of the silent era. Born Gladys Smith, she entered show business as "Baby Gladys," touring in a series of road companies. At age fourteen, a producer gave her the stage name that stuck for Broadway's *The Warrens of Virginia*. The following year she got work as an extra on D.W. Griffith's 1909 film *The Lonely Villa*, and swiftly emerged as a key player in the legendary director's stock company. Her popularity worldwide made her the motion picture industry's first real icon, and she parlayed her success into greater financial rewards and creative control. At age twenty-four, she was Hollywood's first millionaire. Teamed with her swashbuckling husband, Pickford and Douglas Fairbanks were a virtual royal couple leading fairytale lives at their massive Beverly Hills estate, Pickfair.

When Charlie Chaplin, the only other star of a similar magnitude, found himself in the same situation, he teamed up with Pickford and his best friend, Fairbanks to form United Artists in 1919. Transforming herself, Pickford rejected the girlish princess roles and undertook *Rosita* (1923), winning an Academy Award. Soon thereafter, her stardom began to wane. The marriage ended in 1935.

MARY PICKFORD

[1920s; $12-15]

122

Walter Pidgeon

822 HOME OF WALTER PIDGEON

John Hughes Photo

Home of Walter Pidgeon. [c. 1940s; $6-8]

WALTER PIDGEON

Walter Pidgeon (b.1898 - d.1984). A quiet career in banking was abandoned after the death of Walter Pidgeon's first wife. He studied singing at the New England Conservatory of Music and then, in 1924, joined an acting company. His first Broadway appearance was in 1925, and soon thereafter he began work in the silent movies and rose to stardom as Hollywood's "perfect gentleman" for the popular musicals of the early sound era and for dramatic roles that kept him well employed in film and television through the 1970s.

[1930s; $12-15]

Dick Powell and Joan Blondell

841 Residence of Mr. and Mrs. Dick Powell (Joan Blondell), Beverly Hills, California

Home of Dick Powell and Joan Blondell, Beverly Hills. [c. 1940s; $5-7]

First National
DICK POWELL
as Dick Curtis in "Gold Diggers of 1935"

Dick Powell (b.1904 - d.1963). His musical and vocal talents launched Powell on an early career with bands, recording several hit records. He got work as a crooner onscreen in 1932. After a decade of being cast in choir-boy-type leads, he switched to tough-guy hero roles in the 1940s. He went on to frequent television appearances and, in the early '50s, began producing and directing films. He founded the successful Four Star Television company.

Joan Blondell (b.1906 - d.1979). Born to stage comic Eddie Blondell, Joan spent her childhood on the vaudeville circuit. She joined a stock company at age seventeen, and came to New York after winning the Miss Dallas beauty contest. A stage role opposite then-unknown James Cagney in *Penny Arcade* became a film, launching their fame. She appeared in many comedies and musicals type-cast as a dizzy blonde or a gold-digger. She made ten films with Dick Powell, whom she married in 1936. The marriage ended in 1945. She continued in stage and, later, character roles, throughout her life.

JOAN BLONDELL

[1930s; $12-15 each]

Eleanor Powell

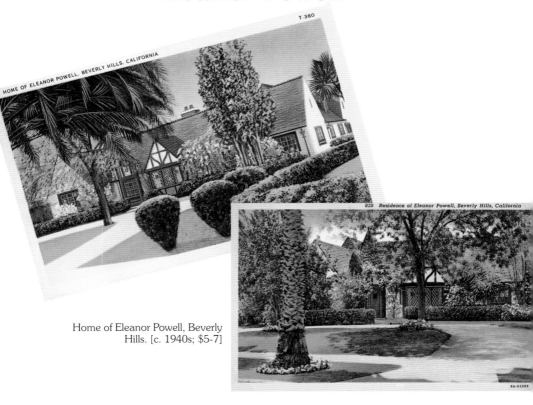

Home of Eleanor Powell, Beverly Hills. [c. 1940s; $5-7]

Eleanor Powell (b.1912 - d.1982). A performer from the age of eleven, Powell debuted in New York as a tap dancer at seventeen years of age and after several Broadway revues landed her first film role in *Scandals* (1935). An outstanding dancer, she retired from film in 1943 when she married actor Glenn Ford. A bitter divorce in 1959 left her financially in need of work, so she revived her career with a well-received Las Vegas nightclub act. She devoted herself to charitable and religious work later in life.

[1930s; $8-10]

William Powell

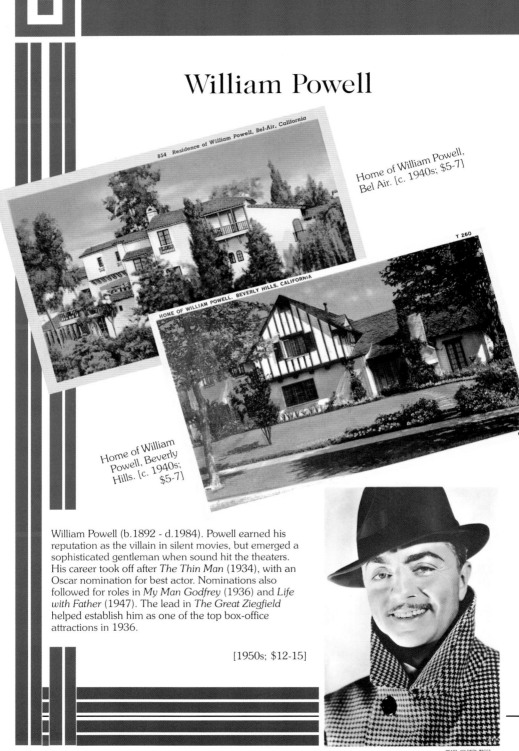

854 Residence of William Powell, Bel-Air, California

Home of William Powell, Bel Air. [c. 1940s; $5-7]

HOME OF WILLIAM POWELL, BEVERLY HILLS, CALIFORNIA

Home of William Powell, Beverly Hills. [c. 1940s; $5-7]

William Powell (b.1892 - d.1984). Powell earned his reputation as the villain in silent movies, but emerged a sophisticated gentleman when sound hit the theaters. His career took off after *The Thin Man* (1934), with an Oscar nomination for best actor. Nominations also followed for roles in *My Man Godfrey* (1936) and *Life with Father* (1947). The lead in *The Great Ziegfield* helped establish him as one of the top box-office attractions in 1936.

[1950s; $12-15]

WILLIAM POWELL   METRO-GOLDWYN-MAYER PICTURES

Tyrone Power

Home of Tyrone Power, Beverly Hills. [c. 1940s; $5-7]

824—Home of Mr. and Mrs. Tyrone Power (Annabella), Brentwood, California

Home of Annabella and Tyrone Power, Brentwood. [c. 1940s; $6-8]

Tyrone Power (b.1914 - d.1958). A lifetime in the theater, beginning at age seven, and stretching through stints as theater usher and related odd jobs, Power remained a bit-part actor until 1936. Cast in a small role in *Girl's Dormitory*, preview audiences reacted so positively that Fox expanded his role for the final release. Power rose to become Fox's top male star, leading almost every major production between 1936 and 1940. After serving in the Marines in World War II, he allowed his popularity to wane while balking at the pretty boy roles and taking on unsympathetic characters. He died of a heart attack on the set of *Solomon and Sheba*.

Luise Rainer

Home of Luise Rainer, Beverly Hills.
[c. 1940s; $5-7]

Luise Rainer (b.1910 - d.). Luise was born in
Vienna. She became an American citizen in
the 1940s, though she now lives in the United
Kingdom. She appeared in Hollywood in
1935 and won two consecutive academy
awards for best actress. She married
playwright Clifford Odets in 1937, but was
divorced three years later. She has a star on
the Hollywood Walk of Fame.

[1930s; $10-12]

LUISE RAINER   METRO-GOLDWYN-MAYER
                         PICTURES

Charles Ray

Home of Charles Ray, Los Angeles.
[c. 1930s; $5-7 each]

..u his Home, Beverly Hills, Calif.

Charles Ray (b.1891 - d.1943). Charles Ray was born in Jacksonville, Illinois. He was an actor, director, writer, and producer. His was typecast as the simple country bumpkin in silent, rural melodramas. A headstrong actor, film producers were hesitant to work with him. He financed a major feature titled *The Courtship of Miles Standish* but the film was a failure that left him penniless. He was unable to make a comeback, possibly due to the introduction of sound pictures.

[1930s; $10-12]

129

Wallace Reid

Home of Wallace Reid, Hollywood. [c. 1930s; $5-7]

Wallace Reid (b.1892 - d.1923). Wallace Reid was born in St. Louis, Missouri, the son of well-known actor and playwright Hal Reid. He started acting as a child before going on to edit for a racecar magazine. He worked as an actor, cameraman, stuntman, and screen-writer. By 1915 he had appeared in more than 100 films. He was labeled the boy-next-door matinee idol. He was most popular when he portrayed a racecar driver. In 1919, he was injured in a train accident that left him addicted to morphine. He died at the age of thirty-one in a rehabiliattion clinic. His wife, Dorothy Davenport, often referring to herself as "Mrs. Wallace Reid," tried to restore his reputation by producing several anti-drug films that included the *Human Wreckage* film in 1923.

Debbie Reynolds

[1950s; $10-12]

Home of Debbie Reynolds, Palm Springs. [c. 1950s; $5-7]

Debbie Reynolds (b.1932 - d.). Debbie Reynolds was born in El Paso, Texas. Her film career began after winning a beauty contest in 1948. As a singer and actress, most of her films were with MGM as perky, wholesome characters. She also headlined in major Las Vegas showrooms. She was nominated for an Academy Award, twice for a Golden Globe, and Blockbuster Entertainment Award. In 1997 she received the Lifetime Achievement Award in Comedy. She has a star on the Hollywood Walk of Fame. She is involved in charity work and dedicated to creating a museum in Hollywood where her extensive collection of costumes, props, and equipment would be housed and exhibited.

Irene Rich

Home of Irene Rich, Hollywood. [c. 1930s; $6-8]

Irene Rich (b.1891 - d.1988). Irene Rich was born in Buffalo, New York. At the age of twenty-seven she began working as a movie extra and went on to star in silent films. After the advent of sound, she frequently played Will Roger's wife. She also was a hit on the radio and had her own show titled *The Irene Rich Show* that lasted for over a decade. She retired in 1950 and married George Henry Clifford. Irene died of heart failure at the age of 96.

[1930s; $15-20]

IRENE RICH - A Warner Bros. Star

Theodore Roberts

799:—Home of Theodore Roberts, Hollywood, Cal.

Home of Theodore Roberts, Hollywood. [c. 1930s; $5-7]

Theodore Roberts (b.1861 - d.1928). Theodore Roberts was born in San Francisco, California. He was nicknamed "The Grand Duke of Hollywood" and is best remembered for his role as Moses in *The Ten Commandments*. He was good friends with Cecil B. De Mille and appeared in twenty-three of his films.

Ginger Rogers

Home of Ginger Rogers, Beverly Hills, Calif.   T596

825   Residence of Ginger Rogers, Beverly Hills, California

Home of Ginger Rogers, Beverly Hills. [c. 1940s; $5-8 each]

Ginger Rogers (b.1911 - d.1995). Ginger Rogers was born in Independence, Missouri. At the age of fourteen, she worked in vaudeville acts until she went to Broadway at age seventeen and appeared in *Top Speed*. She did her first film in 1929. The movie that brought her fame was the 1933 movie *Gold Diggers*. She was often paired in movies with Fred Astaire and they were one of the best cinematic couples to ever to hit the silver screen. She won an Academy Award for her role in *Kitty Foyle*. She retired in 1984. Her autobiography, published in 1991, was called *Ginger, My Story*. She died of natural causes at the age of 83.

[1930s; $15-20]

GINGER ROGERS   UNIVERSAL

Will Rogers

Home of Will Rogers, Beverly Hills. [c. 1930s; $5-7]

Home of Will Rogers, Beverly Hills. [c. 1940s; $5-7]

Home of Will Rogers,
Pacific Palisades
[c. 1930s-40s; $8-10]

WILL ROGERS

AMERICA'S BELOVED COWBOY, HUMORIST,
PHILOSOPHER AND AMBASSADOR OF
GOOD WILL
NOVEMBER 4, 1879 — AUGUST 15, 1935

[1930s-40s; $8-10]

Will Rogers (b.1879 - d.1935). Will Rogers was born in Ooalgah Indian Territory (now Oklahoma). He was a cowboy, world traveler, and circus performer before entering vaudeville. He became a headliner in *Ziegfeld Follies* on Broadway. He made his debut in silent films but became famous with the introduction of sound. He liked to play small town roles that opposed big business, mechanization, and hypocrisy. He was honorary Mayor of Beverly Hills and Acting Mayor of New Orleans. He was even mentioned for Presidency and nominated for Governor of Oklahoma. He actively supported the nomination of Franklin Roosevelt. He was involved in humanitarian acts such as raising money for the 1931 drought and for flood relief. He also donated large amounts of money to numerous charities. He was an expert with horses and the lariat. He died at the age of 55 in a plane crash.

Mickey Rooney

815 HOME OF MICKEY ROONEY. ENCINO. CALIFORNIA

860—Home of Mickey Rooney, Encino, California

Home of Mickey Rooney, Encino.
[c. 1940s; $4-6 each]

Mickey Rooney (b.1920 - d.). Mickey Rooney was born in Brooklyn, New York. He appeared in more than fifty silent movies between 1927 and 1933 as a comic strip character. He reached stardom when he played in the *Andy Hardy* series. He also played opposite Judy Garland in a variety of musicals. He starred in various films from the late 1940s throughout the late 1970s, but made a brilliant comeback in 1980 on Broadway for the musical *Sugar Babies*. His role in the television drama *Bill* won him much acclaim in 1981. He has been married eight times which includes wives Ava Gardner and Martha Vickers. He received the Lifetime Achievement Oscar in 1983.

[1930s; $15-20]

MICKEY ROONEY

Norma Shearer

4A-H2096

Home of Norma Shearer, Beverly Hills. [c. 1940s; $5-7]

Norma Shearer (b.1902 - d.1983). Born in Montreal, Canada, Shearer signed a contract in 1923 with MGM and became a popular actress. Shearer possessed great poise, elegance, and charm. She married producer Irving Thalberg in 1927. She won an Oscar for her role in *The Divorcee* and was nominated for her starring role in *Romeo and Juliet*. After her husband's death in 1936, she lost interest in her career. She turned down the lead role for *Gone With the Wind*. She retired in 1942. Shearer remarried in 1942 and enjoyed forty years with her husband Martin Arrouge. Her brother, Douglas Shearer, was a sound technician who won twelve Oscars for his development of several key technical innovations.

[1930s; $15-20]

Metro-Goldwyn Production

216   NORMA SHEARER

138

Dinah Shore

Dinah Shore's Palm Springs Home

Home of Dinah
Shore, Beverly Hills.
[c. 1950s; $4-6 each]

Dinah Shore (b.1917 - d.1994). Dinah Shore was born in Winchester, Tennessee. Her fame started in the radio business in the early 1940s. In 1943 she began a film career with an all-star musical for the war troops overseas. "I'll Walk Alone" and "Blues in the Night" were some of her popular wartime tunes. She then returned to radio for a period and in 1951 starred in a fifteen minute musical on television. After achieving high ratings and winning Emmys for several consecutive years, she had a very successful award winning television show, *The Dinah Shore Chevy Show*, which ran from 1956-1963. During the 1960s she started a family and was less active in the public eye. She did, however, remain in the Gallup polls as America's most admired woman. She came back to television with *Dinah's Place* (1970-74), *Dinah!* (1974-1979), *Dinah and Friends* (1979-1984), and *A Conversation with Dinah* (1989-91). Her trademark weas to blow a kiss to the audience at the end of her show. She was considered one of television's most popular personalities and helped to pave the way for such talk show hosts as Oprah Winfrey and Sally Jessy Raphael. After divorcing husband George Montgomery, she had a six-year affair with Burt Reynolds, which caused controversy because she was twenty years older than him. She later wrote a series of best-selling cookbooks and sponsored an annual golf tournament.

[1930s; $8-10]

139

Frank Sinatra

Home of Frank Sinatra, Palm Springs.
[c. 1950s; $4-6]

[1940s-50s; $10-12 each]

Frank Sinatra (b.1915 - d.1998). It has been said that he has "the most imitated, most listened to, most recognized voice of the second half of the twentieth century." His career spanned six decades. He launched his career as one of the hugely received Hoboken Four on the *Major Bowes' Amateur Hour*. By 1941, he was voted by Billboard as Best Male Vocalist in 1941. In 1943, he had his first experience with acting. His best films were those where he played boyish charac-

ters, unaware of his charm to women. The role of "Maggio" in the film *From Here to Eternity* won him an Academy Award for Best Supporting Actor. He was part of the "Rat Pack" that included Dean Martin, Sammy Davis Jr., Joey Bishop, and Peter Lawford. He was introduced to John F. Kennedy and they became known as the "Jack Pack." Because of Sinatra's supposed connections with the underworld, President Kennedy began to distance himself from Frank. He had many business ventures that included being Vice-President of the Sands Hotel in Las Vegas, owning a fifty percent share of the Cal-Neva Lodge in Lake Tahoe, investing in a charter airline, music publishing house, restaurants, radio stations, and real estate. He retired briefly in 1971. His accolades include a Grammy Award, the Motion Picture Academy's Jean Hersholt Humanitarian Award for numerous charitable deeds, the Kennedy Center Life Achievement Award, the Presidential Medal of Freedom, a Lifetime Achievement Award from the N.A.A.C.P., and a Congressional Gold Medal for his achievements as a singer, actor, and humanitarian. With more than two hundred recorded collections in print, Sinatra's legacy will live on.

Red Skelton

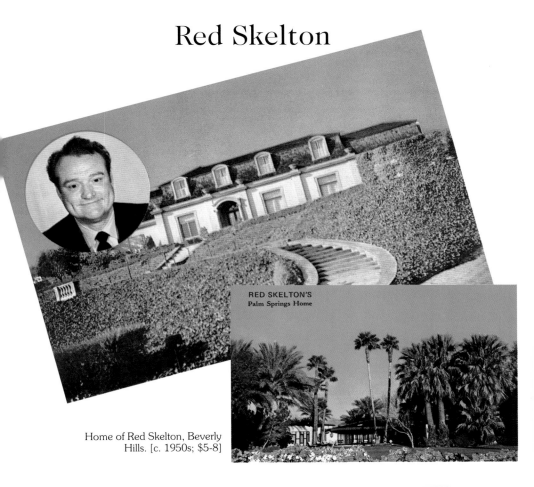

RED SKELTON'S
Palm Springs Home

Home of Red Skelton, Beverly
Hills. [c. 1950s; $5-8]

Red Skelton (b.1913 - d.1997). Red began his career as a
vaudeville and burlesque performer. He started in film in
1938 and appeared in musicals and comedies through the
1940s. His last film was done in 1953. In 1950 he began
in television and earned his fame there. His show *The Red
Skelton Show* ran on NBC, to CBS and back to NBC for a
span of twenty years. His father was in the circus and this
showed in Red's performances as he often wore floppy
hats and comical facial expressions. He always ended the
shows by thanking the audience and saying "God Bless."
In the early 1980s, he did a series of concerts in Carnegie
Hall. He also often did television commercials. He was a
gifted comedian with a passion for corny gags and
slapstick comedy.

[1940s; $8-10]

141

Ann Sothern

Home of Ann Sothern, Beverly Hills. [c. 1950s; $5-7]

Ann Sothern (b.1909 - d. 2001). Ann played small parts in films until she left for Broadway. She came back to Hollywood and acted in B movies, mostly playing the heroine. Her big break came when she played the character Maisie, in a tale about a spirited showgirl and her adventures. It was such a success that she was cast in nine more films playing that character. In the 1950s she had two hit television shows, *Private Secretary* and *The Ann Sothern Show*. She was back in the spotlight in 1987 when she starred in the movie *The Whales of August*, earning an Academy Award nomination.

[1940s; $12-14]

Ann Sothern   Metro-Goldwyn-Mayer

Barbara Stanwyck

Home of Barbara Stanwyck, Los Angeles. [c. 1950s; $5-7]

Barbara Stanwyck (b.1907 - d. 2001). Barbara found her fame on Broadway in *The Noose*. She went on to appear in *Miracle Woman*, *Night Nurse*, and *Woman's Melodrama*. She played gutsy characters in *Annie Oakley* and *Cattle Queen of Montana*. She reached the pinnacle of her career in the 1940s with movies such as *The Lady Eve*, *Ball of Fire*, *Double Indemnity*, and *The Strange Love of Martha Ivers*. During the 1960s she was popular on television with *The Barbara Stanwyck Theatre* and *Big Valley*, for which she won Emmy's for both. She came out of semi-retirement in 1983 to co-star in *The Thorn Birds*, winning another Emmy. During 1985 to 1986 she also co-starred in *Dynasty II: The Colby's*. Most of her roles were about strong-willed, feisty women.

143

James Stewart

Home of James Stewart, Beverly Hills. [c. 1950s; $5-7]

James Stewart (b.1908 - d.1997). James Stewart was born in Indiana, Pennsylvania (where his Oscar resides). He was the son of a local hardware store owner. It has been said that he was "the most complete actor-personality in the American cinema." His fans thought him adorable even though he wasn't "conventionally" handsome because he possessed charisma. Some of his films include *Vivacious Lady* with Ginger Rogers, *Made For Each Other* with Carole Lombard, *Mr. Smith Goes to Washington* with Jean Author, *Destry Rides Again* with Marlene Dietrich, *The Shop Around the Corner*, and *The Mortal Storm*. He won a Best Actor Oscar against competition such as Cary Grant. He joined the Air Force at the age of thirty-three, led 1,000 plane strikes against Germany, and won the Air Medal and Distinguished Flying Cross. He retired from the service as a Brigadier General. After returning from the war he gave his best-known performance in *It's a Wonderful Life* in 1946. He went to Broadway for a time and returned with various movies including *The Greatest Show on Earth*. He won a Best Actor award for his role in *Anatomy of a Murder* in 1959. He was the first actor to earn his salary on a percentage basis, a first for the era of sound movies. He was married in 1949 and had four children.

[1930s; $8-10]

Gloria Swanson

Home of Gloria
Swanson, Beverly Hills.
[c. 1930s; $5-8 each]

Gloria Swanson (b.1899 - d.1983). Gloria was a legend
and considered the prima diva of the silent screen era. She
started her career at Chicago's Essanay Studios in 1913.
She earned fame for her performances in *Male and Female*
in 1919, and *The Affairs of Anatol* in 1921. Her stardom
was at its peak in the mid 1920s when she did *Bluebeard's
Eighth Wife* in 1923, *Zaza* also in 1923, *Madame Sans-
Gene* in 1925, and *The Untamed Lady* in 1926. She
moved on to producing her films and was nominated for an
Oscar as Best Actress. She retired in 1934. She made
attempts to come back thereafter, but wasn't very successful
until her performance in *Sunset Boulevard* which also
earned her another Oscar nomination.

[1930s; $12-15]

Norma Talmadge

853. RESIDENCE OF NORMA TALMADGE, HOLLYWOOD, CALIFORNIA.

NORMA TALMADGE RESIDENCE, 7269 HOLLYWOOD BLVD., HOLLYWOOD, CALIFORNIA   24

Home of Norma Talmadge
[c. 1930s; $5-7]

NORMA TALMADGE

Norma Talmadge (b.1893 - d.1957). Norma was born in Jersey City, New Jersey. She became a star with performances such as *A Tale of Two Cities* in 1911, and *The Battle Cry of Peace* in 1915. She married producer Joseph Schenck in 1917 and they started the Norma Talmadge Film Company, which turned out movies such as *Smilin' Through* in 1922, *Within the Law* in 1923, *Secrets* in 1924, *Kiki* in 1926 which was one of her finest performances, *The Dove* in 1928, and countless others. Her career ended with the introduction of sound films. By that time she was a wealthy woman.

[1930s; $12-15]

Robert Taylor

801   HOME OF ROBERT TAYLOR, NORTHRIDGE ESTATES, CALIF.

HOME OF ROBERT TAYLOR, BEVERLY HILLS, CALIFORNIA

Home of Robert
Taylor [c. 1940s;
$5-8 each]

Robert Taylor (b.1911 - d.1969). Robert Taylor was born in
Nebraska and was signed by MGM while he still attended
school. He was known as the man with the perfect profile.
After starring in *Magnificent Obsession* in 1935, he found
his greatest fame. Some of his films include *Ivanhoe*,
Knights of the Round Table, *The Hangman*, and *Cattle
King*. He was married to Barbara Stanwyck for twelve
years. He died from lung cancer in 1969.

[1930s-40s; $12-15]

Conway Tearle

Home of Conway Tearle [c. 1930s; $5-7]

Conway Tearle (b.1878 - d.1938). Conway was born in New York, New York. He appeared in *Evidence* in 1929, *The Truth About You* in 1930, *The Hurricane Express* in 1932, *Vanity Fair* in 1932, and *Klondike Annie* in 1936.

[1930s; $8-10]

Shirley Temple

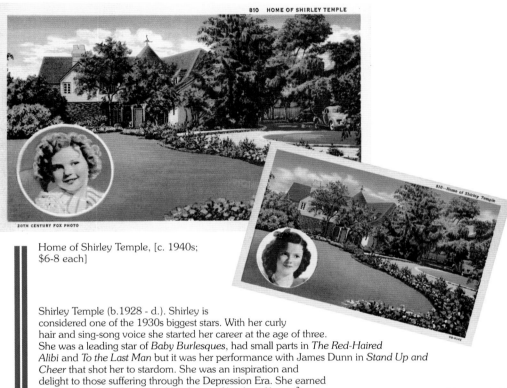

810 HOME OF SHIRLEY TEMPLE

20TH CENTURY FOX PHOTO

810—Home of Shirley Temple

Home of Shirley Temple, [c. 1940s; $6-8 each]

Shirley Temple (b.1928 - d.). Shirley is considered one of the 1930s biggest stars. With her curly hair and sing-song voice she started her career at the age of three. She was a leading star of *Baby Burlesques*, had small parts in *The Red-Haired Alibi* and *To the Last Man* but it was her performance with James Dunn in *Stand Up and Cheer* that shot her to stardom. She was an inspiration and delight to those suffering through the Depression Era. She earned a special Juvenile Oscar in 1934. Some of her best films are *Bright Eyes*, *The Littlest Colonel*, *The Littlest Rebel*, and *Dimples*. By 1937 she was the number one actress in America and this success continued for the next three years. As she began to get older, the public and film producers started losing interest. By the 1950 her career in film was essentially over. She then moved to television and starred in *Shirley Temple's Storybook*, a series on ABC that consisted of sixteen specials. Her next move was to NBC in show titled *The Shirley Temple Show*. She then retired to raise her family. Her 1967 bid for a Republican seat in the US Congress was unsuccessful, but in 1968 Richard Nixon appointed her US Ambassador to the United Nations. She was US Ambassador to Ghana and later was US Chief of Protocol. Her political career lasted into the early 1990s. Her memoirs, called *Child Star*, was published in 1988.

[1930s; $25-30]

Shirley Temple

Danny Thomas

Home of Danny
Thomas, Beverly Hills.
[c. 1950s; $5-7 each]

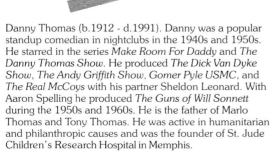

Danny Thomas (b.1912 - d.1991). Danny was a popular
standup comedian in nightclubs in the 1940s and 1950s.
He starred in the series *Make Room For Daddy* and *The
Danny Thomas Show*. He produced *The Dick Van Dyke
Show*, *The Andy Griffith Show*, *Gomer Pyle USMC*, and
The Real McCoys with his partner Sheldon Leonard. With
Aaron Spelling he produced *The Guns of Will Sonnett*
during the 1950s and 1960s. He is the father of Marlo
Thomas and Tony Thomas. He was active in humanitarian
and philanthropic causes and was the founder of St. Jude
Children's Research Hospital in Memphis.

[1940s; $8-10]

Ernest Torrence

RESIDENCE OF ERNEST TORRENCE, HOLLYWOOD, LOS ANGELES, CALIFORNIA

Home of Ernest Torrence, Hollywood. [c. 1930s; $5-7]

Ernest Torrence (b.1878 - d.1933). Ernest was born in Edinburgh, Scotland. He is the older brother to actor David Torrence. He began his career in opera. When his voice began to fail him, he turned to silent films. Some of his memorable roles were in *Tol'able David*, *Peter Pan*, *Sherlock Holmes*, and *I Cover the Waterfront*.

Rudolph Valentino

820:—Rudolph Valentino Home, Whitley Heights, Hollywood, Calif.

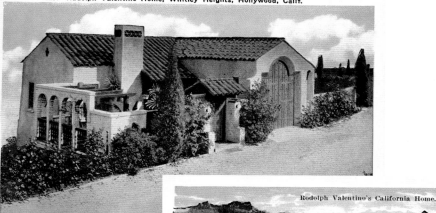

Home of Rudolph
Valentino, Whitley
Heights, Hollywood.
[c. 1930s; $5-7]

Rudolph Valentino's California Home.

Rudolph Valentino (b.1895 - d.1926). Rudolph was born in Italy and came to the United States as a teenager. He was adored by the ladies because of his exotic good looks and his erotic charisma. He was dubbed the original "Latin Lover" and was one of silent films most famed stars. He started out in films with small parts but soon a screenwriter saw his potential and landed him the lead role in *Four Horsemen of the Apocalypse* in 1921. This film shot him to stardom. Some of Valentino's major roles were in the films *The Sheik* in 1921, *Monsieur Beaucaire* in 1923, *The Eagle* in 1925, and *The Son of the Sheik* in 1926. His death at the age of thirty-one due to a perforated ulcer caused riots and alleged suicides among his female fans.

Rudolph Valentino

[1930s; $25-30]

Lupe Velez

T133

LUPE VELEZ'S HOME, BEVERLY HILLS, CALIFORNIA

Home of Lupe Velez, Beverly Hills.
[c. 1930s; $5-7]

Lupe Velez (b.1908 - d.1944). Born in San Luis Potosi, Mexico, she was nicknamed "The Mexican Spitfire" and "The Hot Pepper" because of her stunning beauty. She started as a chorus girl in *The Music Box Review* in the late 1920s. In 1929 she appeared in four movies including *Wolf Song*, co-starring with Gary Cooper, her fiancé at the time. She starred in *The Half-Naked Truth* in 1932 and this opened the door for her to do comedy. Her love life was always high-profile with men such as Gary Cooper, John Gilbert, Charlie Chaplin, Jack Dempsey, Victor Fleming, and others. The year 1944 found her pregnant and unwed to the baby's father. She committed suicide, reportedly drowning herself in a toilet, however physically impossible that seems.

[1930s; $8-10]

LUPE VELEZ   METRO GOLDWYN MAYER PICTURES

Florence Vidor

824:—King-Florence Vidor's Home, Hollywood, Calif.

17598

Home of Florence Vidor, Hollywood. [c. 1930s; $5-7]

Florence Vidor (b.1895 - d.1977). Born in Houston, Texas, she and her Texan husband, King Vidor moved into their Model T and self-financed a trip to Hollywood to start movie careers. Florence first garnered attention for her role in *A Tale of Two Cities* in 1917. In 1919 her husband opened his own studio and rose to the top of the director ladder. Florence became a major star in movies such as *Alice Adams*, *The Marriage Circle*, and *Barbara Frietchie*. Her first sound film, also her last, was *Chinatown Nights* in 1929. She retired and married a second time to violinist Jascha Heifetz.

Loretta Young

Home of Loretta Young, Belair.
[c. 1940s; $5-8]

Loretta Young (b.1913 - d. 2000). Loretta had small bits in film at the age of three and reappeared at the age of fourteen playing a role in *Naughty But Nice* in 1927. By the mid 1930s she was one of the more prominent leading ladies. She was often given parts in film because of her beauty and personality more than her talent. She reached the peak of her career in the late 1940s with such films as *The Bishop's Wife*, *The Farmer's Daughter* that won her an Oscar nomination, *Rachel and the Stranger*, and *Come to the Stable* that won her Best Actress Oscar. In 1954 she had her own show called *The Loretta Young Show* that ran until 1963. After the show ended she retired. Twenty five years later she came back to appear in two television movies, *Christmas Eve* in 1986 and *Lady in a Corner* in 1989. Her daughter wrote a book in which she said she had been born out of wedlock to father Clark Gable. She said her mother led her to believe for years that she had been adopted.

[1940s; $12-15]

155

Lawrence Welk

Lawrence Welk's Indian Wells Home

Home of Lawrence Welk, Maitou Springs. [c. 1950s; $5-7]

Lawrence Welk (b.1903 - d.1992). Lawrence Welk was raised in a German speaking family and didn't learn English until he was twenty-one, which explains his accent. In the late 1930s, he succeeded in radio with his "Biggest Little Band in America." His music was labeled "Champagne Music" after listeners would call in and say his music reminded them of "sipping champagne." His band went on to television in the early 1950s and went nationwide. His show was cancelled in 1971, but he earned more financial wealth in the following eleven years from syndication than he earned during his sixteen years with the show. He continued to tour up until his eighties.

[1930s-40s; $8-10]

Jane Withers

Homes of Jane Withers,
Westwood. [c. 1940s;
$5-8 each]

807—Home of Jane Withers, Westwood, California

62683

1B-H137

Homes of Jane Withers,
Westwood. [c. 1940s; $5-8 each]

Jane Withers (b.1926 - d.). At age four she was starring on her own radio show in Atlanta. She came to Hollywood playing opposite Shirley Temple in *Bright Eyes* in 1934. As a child star, she played in forty-seven films. She has had roles in so many films they are too numerous to name. Television viewers of the 1960s and 1970s will remember her commercials as the plumber for Comet cleanser. She is an avid collector of dolls and teddy bears, for which someday she hopes to build a museum. She has developed a non-profit organization that helps girls and young women to attain their goals.

Jane Wyman

Home of Jane Wyman, Beverly Hills. [c. 1950s; $5-7]

Jane Wyman (b.1914 - d.) Jane was an actress in low budget films when she started her acting career. It was her performance in *The Lost Weekend* in 1945 that brought her recognition. She was nominated for four Oscars, one of which she won for her performance in *Johnny Belinda* in 1948 where she played a deaf-mute rape victim. She was host of *The Jane Wyman Theatre* in the mid 1950s. Her popularity started to decline, but she continued to make films. In 1960 she played in the Disney movie *Pollyana*. She then took a break and came back making movies for television. She then moved on to playing the character Angela Channing on *Falcon Crest* that aired on CBS. The program ran from 1981 until 1990. She was married to Ronald Reagan in 1940. Their marriage lasted until 1948. Their daughter, Maureen Regan, is a singer-actress.

Jane Wyman plays an American Airlines stewardess in MGM's "Three Guys Named Mike".

[c. 1940s; $15-20]

159

Valuing Postcards

The values shown in this book are provided as a guideline for collectors and dealers. The values are based upon rarity of the postcard views. Condition has not been factored in and should be considered when evaluating individual postcards.

A Short History of the Postcard in the United States

Pioneer Era (1893-1898)
Although there were earlier scattered issues, most pioneer cards in today's collections begin with the cards placed on sale at the Columbian Exposition in Chicago, Illinois, on May 1, 1893. These were illustrations on government printed postal cards and privately printed souvenir cards. The government postal cards had the printed one-cent stamp, while the souvenir cards required a two-cent adhesive postage stamp to be applied. Writing was not permitted on the address side of the cards.

Private Mailing Card Era (1898-1901)
On May 19, 1898, private printers were granted permission, by an act of Congress, to print and sell cards that bore the inscription "Private Mailing Card." Today, we call these cards "PMCs." Postage required was now a one-cent adhesive stamp. A dozen or more American printers began to take postcards seriously. Writing was still not permitted on the address side.

Postcard Era (1901-1907)
The use of the word "Postcard" was granted by the government to private printers on December 24, 1901. Writing was still not permitted on the address side. In this era, private citizens began to take black-and-white photographs and have them printed on paper with postcard backs.

Divided Back Era (1907-1914)
Postcards with a divided back were permitted March 1, 1907. The address was to be written on the right side and the left side was for writing messages. Many millions of cards were published and printed in this era, most in Germany, where printers were far more advanced in the lithographic processes. With the advent of World War I, the supply of postcards had to come from England and the United States.

White Border Era (1915-1930)
Most domestic-use postcards were printed in the United States during this period. To save ink, a border was left around the view, thus the name "White Border Cards." The high cost of labor, inexperience, and public taste created cards of inferior quality. Competition in a narrowing market caused many publishers to go out of business.

Linen Era (1930-1944)
New printing processes allowed printing on postcards with high rag content that caused a linen-like finish. These inexpensive cards allowed for the use of gaudy dyes for coloring. Curt Teich's line of linen postcards flourished. Many important historical events are recorded on these cards.

Photochrome Era (1945 to present)
The chrome postcards started to dominate the scene soon after they were launched by the Union Oil Company in their western service stations in 1939. Mike Roberts pioneered with his "WESCO" cards soon after World War II. Three-dimensional postcards also appeared during this era.